SIDE by SIDE

ACTIVITY WORKBOOK

Second Edition

1

Steven J. Molinsky

Bill Bliss

with

Carolyn Graham

Contributing Authors

Elizabeth Handley with *Mary Ann Perry* and *Christine Harvey*

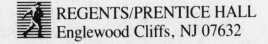
REGENTS/PRENTICE HALL
Englewood Cliffs, NJ 07632

Editorial/production supervision: Janet Johnston
Art supervision: Jerry Votta, Karen Salzbach
Manufacturing buyers: Laura Crossland, Peter Havens
Cover design: Kenny Beck

Illustrated by Richard E. Hill

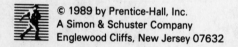 © 1989 by Prentice-Hall, Inc.
A Simon & Schuster Company
Englewood Cliffs, New Jersey 07632

Printed in the United States of America

10   9

ISBN 0-13-811696-2

Prentice-Hall International (UK) Limited, *London*
Prentice-Hall of Australia Pty. Limited, *Sydney*
Prentice-Hall Canada Inc., *Toronto*
Prentice-Hall Hispanoamericana, S.A., *Mexico*
Prentice-Hall of India Private Limited, *New Delhi*
Prentice-Hall of Japan, Inc. *Tokyo*
Simon & Schuster Asia Pte. Ltd., *Singapore*
Editora Prentice-Hall do Brasil, Ltda., *Rio de Janeiro*

CONTENTS

A. WHAT ARE THEY SAYING?

what's	my	name	from
is	your	address	you
I'm		phone number	

1. What's your name?

My ___name___ ___is___ Betty Jones.

2. _____ _____
   address?

   _____ _____
   _____ 333 Main Street.

3. _____ _____
   phone number?

   _____ _____
   _____ _____ 868–2766.

4. _____ _____ name?

My name _____.

Harry Ross
10 River Street

5. _____ _____
   address?

My _____ _____
_____ _____ _____.

6.

_____ _____ _____ _____?

My phone number _____ 723–1576.

7.

Where are _____ from?

_____ _____ Chicago.

B. NAME/ADDRESS/PHONE NUMBER

What's YOUR name, address, and phone number?

STUDENT IDENTIFICATION CARD
Name: _Maria_   _Gonzalez_   First Name   Last Name
Address: _235 Main Street_
Bronx, New York
Phone Number: _741–8906_

STUDENT IDENTIFICATION CARD
Name: _____   First Name   Last Name
Address: _____
_____
Phone Number: _____

My name is Maria Gonzalez.
My address is 235 Main Street.
My phone number is 741–8906.

_My_ ...... _name_ ...... _is_ ....

....

....

one	two	three	four	five	six	seven	eight	nine	ten

C. WRITE

1 = _____one_____

2 = _____

3 = _____

4 = _____

5 = _____

6 = _____

7 = _____

8 = _____

9 = _____

10 = _____

D. WHAT'S THE NUMBER?

1. My address is four Main Street.

2. My address is ten Main Street.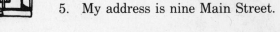

3. My address is seven Main Street.

4. My address is five Main Street.

5. My address is nine Main Street.

6. My address is eight Main Street.

E. LISTEN

Listen and write the missing number.

1. What's your phone number? / My phone number is 231–496 _5_ .

2. What's your phone number? / My phone number is 743–529 ___ .

3. What's your phone number? / My phone number is 492–71 ___ 5.

4. What's your phone number? / My phone number is 637–89 ___ 6.

F. LISTEN

Listen and put a circle around the number you hear.

1. | 1 | ③ | 5 |

2. | 6 | 7 | 8 |

3. | 4 | 5 | 6 |

4. | 5 | 7 | 10 |

5. | 6 | 8 | 9 |

6. | 2 | 3 | 6 |

3

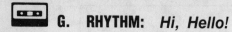 **G. RHYTHM:** *Hi, Hello!*

Listen. Then clap and practice.

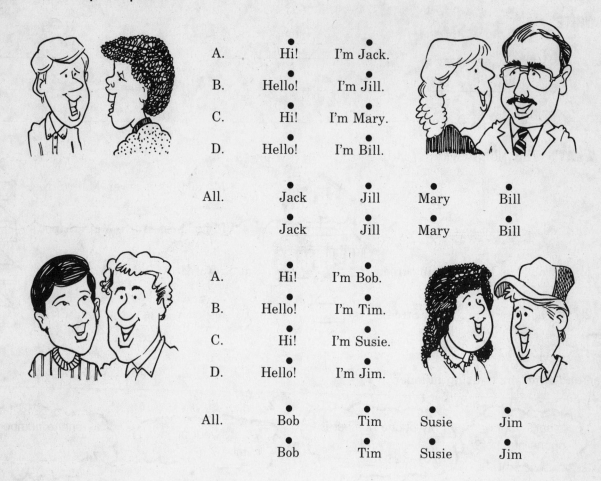

A.	Hi!	I'm Jack.
B.	Hello!	I'm Jill.
C.	Hi!	I'm Mary.
D.	Hello!	I'm Bill.

All.	Jack	Jill	Mary	Bill
	Jack	Jill	Mary	Bill

A.	Hi!	I'm Bob.
B.	Hello!	I'm Tim.
C.	Hi!	I'm Susie.
D.	Hello!	I'm Jim.

All.	Bob	Tim	Susie	Jim
	Bob	Tim	Susie	Jim

H. INTONATION: *Happy Greetings*

1. **Listen and repeat.**

2. **In groups of four, practice happy greetings.**

Sue! Jim! Ellen! Tim!   Mary! Dan! Jack! Ann!

Al! Sal! Bill! Jill!   Ellen! Helen! Lou! Sue!

_____! _____! _____! _____!

(Use your own names)

4

A. WHAT ARE THEY SAYING?

I'm	you	basement	living room
we're	are	bedroom	yard
they're	where	kitchen	

1.
Where are you?

_I'm_ in the garage.

2.
Where _____ you?

We're in the _____.

3.
_____ _____ Harry and Betty?

They're in the _____.

4.
_____ you and Tom?

_____ in the _____.

5.
Where _____ John and Bill?

_____ in the _____.

6.
_____ _____ you?

_____ in the _____.

B. WHAT ARE THEY SAYING?

where's	she's	living room	kitchen
he's	it's	garage	

Where's Fred?

He's in the *kitchen*.

_____ Helen?

_____ in the _____ _____.

_____ the car?

_____ in the _____

1.

2.

3.

C. WHERE ARE THEY?

we	he	they
	she	
	it	

(Mr. and Mrs Jones) 1. _____ *They* _____ are in the dining room.

(Helen) 2. _____ is in the living room.

(Mr. Nelson) 3. _____ is in the bedroom.

(Fred and Tom) 4. _____ are in the attic.

(Betty and I) 5. _____ are in the garage.

(The newspaper) 6. _____ is in the bedroom.

(John) 7. _____ is in the bathroom.

(Mrs. Wilson) 8. _____ is in the basement.

(The cat) 9. _____ is in the yard.

D. WHERE ARE THEY?

I'm	we're	he's	where's
	you're	she's	
	they're	it's	

(He is) 1. _____ *He's* _____ in the garage.

(I am) 2. _____ in the kitchen.

(We are) 3. _____ in the bedroom.

(You are) 4. _____ in the dining room.

(She is) 5. _____ in the living room.

(Where is) 6. _____ the newspaper?

(It is) 7. _____ in the basement.

(They are) 8. _____ in the yard.

6

E. THE FRANKLIN FAMILY

The Franklin family is at home today. (1) Mr. Franklin is ___in___ ___the___ ___kitchen___ .

(2) Mrs. Franklin is _____ _____ _____ . (3) Tom and Jane are _____ _____

_____ _____ . (4) Betty _____ _____ _____ _____ .

(5) The dog _____ _____ _____ _____ _____ . (6) The cat _____ _____

_____ _____ .

F. WHERE ARE THEY?

he's	they're
she's	
it's	

1. Where's Mr. Franklin?   _____ _He's in the kitchen._ _____

2. Where's Mrs. Franklin?   _____

3. Where are Tom and Jane? _____

4. Where's Betty?   _____

5. Where's the dog?   _____

6. Where's the cat?   _____

7

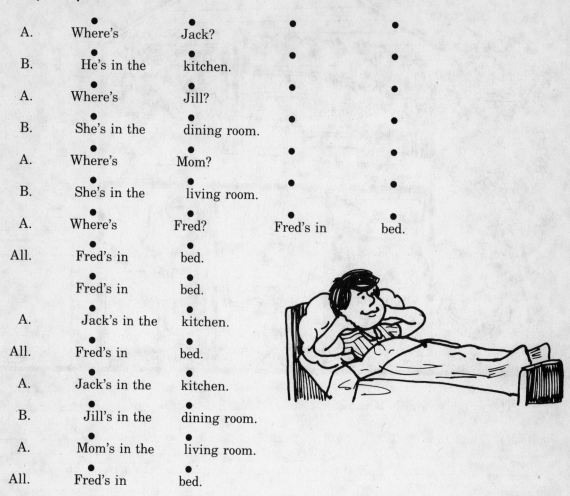

G. RHYTHM: *Where's Jack?*

Listen.   Then clap and practice.

A.	Where's	Jack?		
B.	He's in the	kitchen.		
A.	Where's	Jill?		
B.	She's in the	dining room.		
A.	Where's	Mom?		
B.	She's in the	living room.		
A.	Where's	Fred?	Fred's in	bed.
All.	Fred's in	bed.		
	Fred's in	bed.		
A.	Jack's in the	kitchen.		
All.	Fred's in	bed.		
A.	Jack's in the	kitchen.		
B.	Jill's in the	dining room.		
A.	Mom's in the	living room.		
All.	Fred's in	bed.		

H. PRONUNCIATION: *Where Are Fred and Mary?*

Listen.   Then clap and practice.

> Where are = Whére're   Fred and Mary = Fred 'n Mary

A.	Where's	Jack?	A.	Jack and	Jill.
B.	Where's	Jill?	B.	Betty and	Bill.
C.	Where are Fred and	Mary?	C.	Bob and	Lou.
D.	Where's	Bill?	D.	Mary and	Sue.
A.	Where's	Ed?	A.	Jack and	Jill.
B.	Where's	Sue?	B.	Betty and	Bill.
C.	Where are Bob and	Betty?	C.	Bob and	Lou.
D.	Where are Tom and Lou?		D.	Mary and	Sue.

I. WHAT'S THE SIGN?

Fill in the signs. Then complete the sentences.

1. Tom and Mary are _____*in the library*_____.

2. Albert is _____

_____.

3. Fred and Helen are _____

_____.

4. Betty _____

_____.

5. Rita _____

_____.

6. Bob and Jane _____

_____.

7. Jane _____

_____.

8. John and Martha _____

_____.

Listen to each sentence.   Put a check (✔) next to the appropriate picture.

🔊 **K. LISTEN**

Listen to the following conversations.   Put a circle around the right word.

1. Where are ⎡ zoo / (you) ⎤ ?

2. I'm in the ⎡ car / yard ⎤ with ⎡ Mr. / Mrs. ⎤ Jones.

3. Where's ⎡ Mr. / Mrs. ⎤ Jones?

4. ⎡ He's / She's ⎤ in Mexico City.

5. ⎡ Where / We ⎤ are you?

6. ⎡ I / I'm ⎤ in the ⎡ bathroom / bedroom ⎤

7. ⎡ Where's / Where ⎤ the newspaper?

8. ⎡ Is / It's ⎤ in the living room.

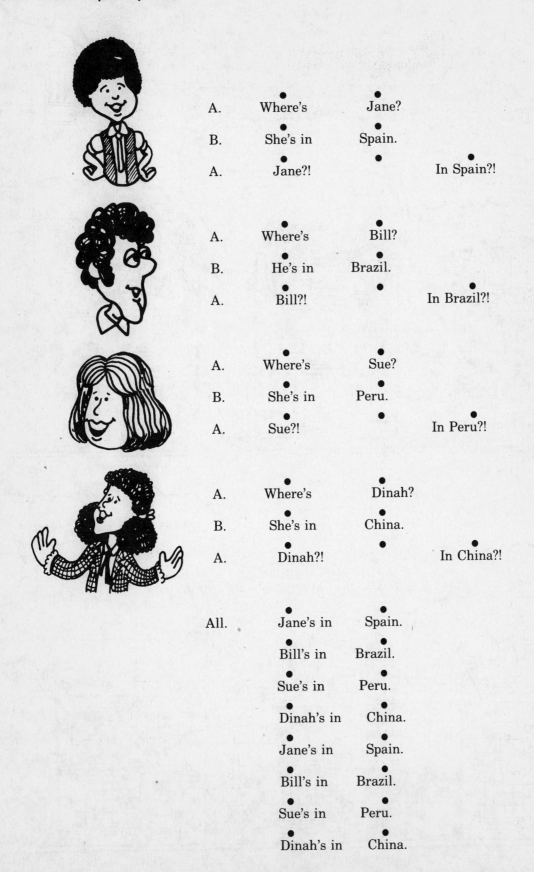

L. INTONATION: *Jane?! In Spain?!*

Listen. Then clap and practice.

A.   Where's   Jane?
B.   She's in   Spain.
A.   Jane?!   In Spain?!

A.   Where's   Bill?
B.   He's in   Brazil.
A.   Bill?!   In Brazil?!

A.   Where's   Sue?
B.   She's in   Peru.
A.   Sue?!   In Peru?!

A.   Where's   Dinah?
B.   She's in   China.
A.   Dinah?!   In China?!

All.   Jane's in   Spain.
Bill's in   Brazil.
Sue's in   Peru.
Dinah's in   China.
Jane's in   Spain.
Bill's in   Brazil.
Sue's in   Peru.
Dinah's in   China.

11

A. WHAT ARE THEY SAYING?

doing	I'm	you
cooking	he's	the dog
sleeping	she's	what
studying	it's	what's
watching	they're	are

3

1.
_What__ are you doing?

_I'm__ reading.

2.
What _____ _____ doing?

We're

_____.

3.
What _____ Mary and Fred

_____?

_____

_____

English.

4.
What's Tom _____?

_____ eating.

5.
_____

Martha _____?

_____

_____ TV.

6.
What's _____ _____

_____?

_____

_____.

12

B. WHAT ARE THEY DOING?

dancing	listening	singing
drinking	playing	sleeping
eating	reading	watching

1. He's ___*reading*___ .

2. She's _____ .

3. They're _____ .

4. He's _____ .

5. She's _____ to the radio.

6. They're _____ cards.

7. He's _____ .

8. They're _____ coffee.

9. She's _____ TV.

Listen.   Then clap and practice.

What's he = Whátsee   Where are = Whére're   What are = Whát're

A.	Where's	Charlie?		
B.	He's in the	kitchen.		
A.	What's he	doing?		
B.	Eating	lunch.		
All.	Charlie's in the	kitchen	eating	lunch.
	Charlie's in the	kitchen	eating	lunch.
A.	Who's <u>in</u> the	kitchen?		
B.	Charlie's in the	kitchen.		
A.	What's he	doing?		
B.	Eating	lunch.		

A.	Where's	Betty?
B.	She's in the	bedroom.
A.	What's she	doing?
B.	Reading a	book.

All.   Betty's in the   bedroom   reading a   book.

Betty's in the   bedroom   reading a   book.

A.   Who's in the   bedroom?

B.   Betty's in the   bedroom.

A.   What's she   doing?

B.   Reading a   book.

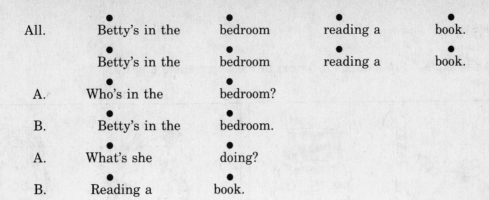

A.   Where are Mom and Dad?

B.   They're in the   living room.

A.   What are they   doing?

B.   Watching Channel   Seven.

All.   Betty's in the   bedroom.

Mom's in the   living room.

Dad's in the   living room.

Charlie's in the   kitchen.

A.   Where's   Charlie?

All.   He's in the   kitchen.

A.   What's he   doing?

All.   Eating   lunch.

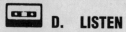
Listen to each sentence.   Put a check (✔) next to the appropriate picture.

E. WHAT'S THE QUESTION?

Where is $\left\{ \begin{array}{l} \text{he} \\ \text{she} \\ \text{it} \end{array} \right\}$?   What's $\left\{ \begin{array}{l} \text{he} \\ \text{she} \\ \text{it} \end{array} \right\}$ doing?

Where are $\left\{ \begin{array}{l} \text{you} \\ \text{they} \end{array} \right\}$?   What are $\left\{ \begin{array}{l} \text{you} \\ \text{they} \end{array} \right\}$ doing?

1. _Where_ _are_ _you_ ?   I'm in the bedroom.

2. _What's_ _she_ _doing_ ?   She's playing cards.

3. _____ _____ _____ ?   He's in the night club.

4. _____ ?   I'm studying English.

5. _____ ?   He's eating breakfast.

6. _____ ?   They're in the bank.

7. _____ ?   We're in the library.

8. _____ ?   It's in the garage.

9. _____ ?   She's in the park.

10. _____ ?   It's sleeping.

11. _____ ?   They're playing baseball.

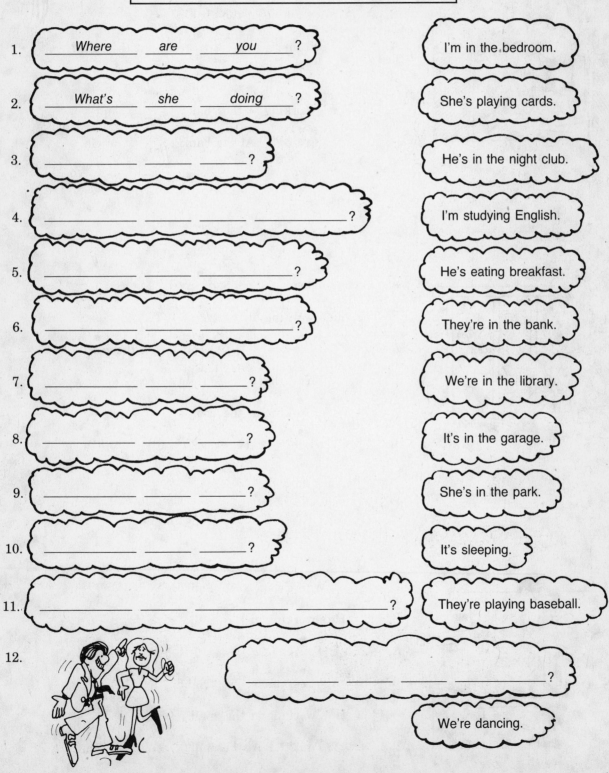

12. _____ ?

We're dancing.

17

Listen. Then clap and practice.

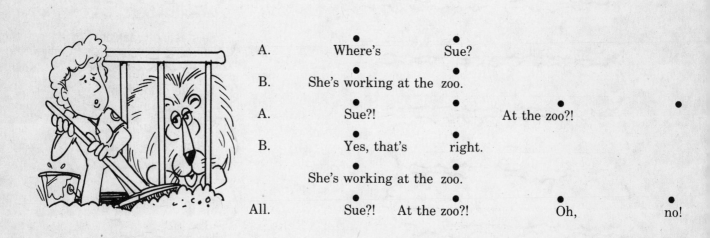

A. Where's Frank?

B. He's working at the bank.

A. Frank?! At the bank?!

B. Yes, that's right.
He's working at the bank.

All. Frank?! At the bank?! Oh, no!

A. Where's Sue?

B. She's working at the zoo.

A. Sue?! At the zoo?!

B. Yes, that's right.
She's working at the zoo.

All. Sue?! At the zoo?! Oh, no!

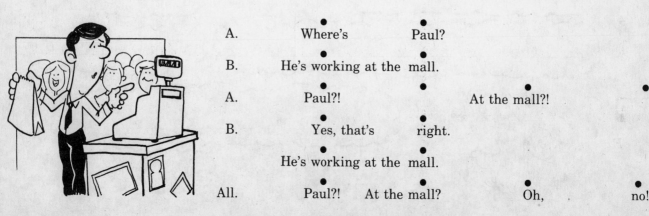

A. Where's Paul?

B. He's working at the mall.

A. Paul?! At the mall?!

B. Yes, that's right.
He's working at the mall.

All. Paul?! At the mall? Oh, no!

CHECK-UP TEST: *Chapters 1–3*

A. Answer the questions.

Ex. What's your telephone number?

My ....*telephone number is 236–2558*.... .

1. What's your name?

My ....

2. What's your address?

My ....

3. Where are you from?

I ....

B. Put a circle around the correct answer.

Ex. The car is in the

| (garage) |
| hospital |
| supermarket |

1. Walter is eating

| restaurant |
| coffee |
| breakfast |

2. Where's Tom?

| He's |
| You're |
| She's |

in the bedroom.

3. The monkey is in the

| bank |
| post office |
| zoo |

4. Where are you?

| They're |
| We're |
| He's |

in the living room.

5. Albert is in the library.

He's

| cooking |
| dancing |
| reading |

6. Miss Jackson is drinking

| dining room |
| cafeteria |
| coffee |

7. Jane is playing

| cards |
| car |
| yard |

C. Fill in the blanks.

Ex. They're ___*in*___ the bedroom.

1. _____ are you?   I'm in the yard.

2. What's Helen _____?   She's sleeping.

3. Tom is _____ the garage.

4. What's Miss Jones doing?   _____ singing.

5. Where's the newspaper?   _____ in the kitchen.

6. Walter _____ Mary are in the bank.

7. She's _____ TV.

8. Bobby is _____ to the radio.

9. _____ are Mr. and Mrs. Smith doing?

10. Where are you and Tom?   _____ in the park.

D. Listen and write the number you hear.

Ex. 547-2_6_31

1. 695–33__2

2. 49___–8577

3. 7__4–0681

4. 358–967___

5. 582–41__6

A. ON THE PHONE

what	her	my	cleaning	children
what's	his	our	doing	homework
are		their	fixing	sink

1.
Hi! ___*What*___ are you doing?

I'm fixing ___*my*___ ___*sink*___ .

2.
What's Bob _____?

He's _____ _____ car.

3.
_____ Mary doing?

She's cleaning _____ room.

4.
_____ _____ you doing?

We're _____

_____ apartment.

5.
What are your _____ doing?

They're doing _____ .

20

B. WHAT'S THE WORD?

my	our
his	your
her	their
its	

1. I'm fixing _____*my*_____ sink.

2. We're cleaning _____ yard.

3. Nancy is washing _____ car.

4. Mr. and Mrs. Jones are doing _____ exercises.

5. Henry is feeding _____ cat.

6. The dog is eating _____ dinner.

7. You're doing _____ homework.

C. PUZZLE

Across

3. Albert is brushing _____ teeth.

5. You're fixing _____ bicycle.

7. Maria is cleaning _____ room.

Down

1. The cat is eating _____ breakfast.

2. Mr. and Mrs. Thompson are painting _____ living room.

4. I'm washing _____ hair.

6. We're washing _____ windows.

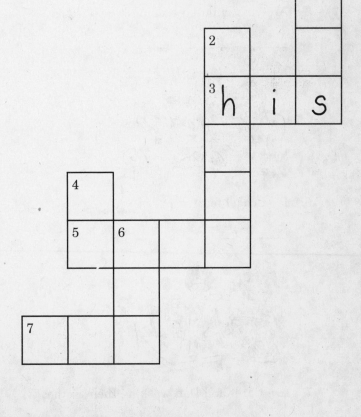

D. SHORT ANSWERS

Yes, I am.	Yes, $\begin{Bmatrix} he \\ she \\ it \end{Bmatrix}$ is.	Yes, $\begin{Bmatrix} we \\ you \\ they \end{Bmatrix}$ are.

1. Is Peggy fixing her car?

   Yes,   *she*   *is.*

2. Are you painting your living room?

   _____ _____ _____

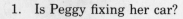

3. Are your children cooking breakfast?

   _____ _____ _____

4. Are you and John cleaning the garage?

   _____ _____ _____

5. Is Michael feeding his cat?

   _____ _____ _____

6. Am I doing my homework?

   _____ _____ _____

7. Are Carol and Dan washing their clothes?

   _____ _____ _____

8. Is Mrs. McDonald doing her exercises?

   _____ _____ _____

E. RHYTHM AND RHYME: *Busy! Busy! Busy!*

Listen. Then clap and practice.

What are = Whát're	Is ~~he~~ = Izzy	Yes, ~~he~~ = Yéssee	What's ~~he~~ = Whátsee

A.   Are you busy?

B.   Yes, I   am.

A.   What are you   doing?

B.   I'm talking to   Sam.

A.   Is he busy?

B.   Yes, he   is.

A.   What's he   doing?

B.   He's talking to   Liz.

A.   Are they busy?

B.   Yes, they   are.

A.   What are they   doing?

B.   They're washing their car.

All.   Am!   Sam!

        Is!   Liz!

        Are!   Car!

        Busy! Busy! Busy!

F. WHAT ARE THEY DOING?

1. He's _____feeding_____

   his _____dog_____ .

2. They're _____

   their _____ .

3. He's _____

   his _____ .

4. She's _____

   her _____ _____ .

5. He's _____

   his _____ .

6. He's _____

   his _____ .

G. WHAT'S THE WORD?

Put a circle around the correct word.

1. | Where / We're | are you and Betty?

2. | Where / We're | in | our / are | room.

3. What are you doing?

   We're | washing / watching | TV.

4. | Is / His | Sam busy?

5. Yes, he is. | He's / His | cleaning | he's / his | room.

6. | Are / Our | Jane and Mark busy?

7. Yes, they are. | They're / Their | fixing | they're / their | car.

8. Where's the dog?

   | It's / Its | in the kitchen. | It's / Its | eating | its / it's | breakfast.

H. A BUSY DAY IN ROCKVILLE

restaurant	fixing	what's	his	Mr.	clothes
library	playing	where's	her	Mrs.	newspaper
night club	studying	they're	are	Miss	bicycle
laundromat					

(1) It's a busy day in Rockville. (2) Mr. and Mrs. Green are in the _____*restaurant*_____.

(3) _____ eating dinner. (4) Charlie Harris is in the _____. (5) He's

_____ the piano.

(6) Mr. and _____ Sharp are in the _____. (7) They're washing

their _____.

(8) _____ Nathan is reading the _____, and Mr. Rinaldi is doing

_____ exercises.

(9) Patty Williams and _____ Johnson _____ in the parking lot. (10) Patty is

_____ her _____. (11) _____ Johnson is washing _____ car.

(12) _____ Bobby Davis? (13) He's in the _____.

(14) _____ he doing? (15) He's _____ mathematics.

I. RHYTHM: *Practicing English*

Listen.   Then clap and practice.

What's he = Whátsee	Where's he = Whérzee

All.   Practicing   English   all the   time!

Practicing, practicing, practicing, practicing!

Practicing   English   all the   time!

Practicing, practicing, practicing, practicing!

A.   Practicing   English   in the kitchen,

B.   Practicing   English   in the park,

C.   Practicing   English   in the restaurant,

D.   Practicing   English   in the dark!

All.   What's he   doing?

A.   Practicing   English.

Practicing   English   all the   time!

All.   Practicing, practicing, practicing, practicing!

Practicing   English   all the   time!

A.   Where's he practicing?

All.   In the   kitchen.

B.   Where's he practicing?

All.   In the   park.

C.   Where's he practicing?

All.   In the   restaurant.

D.   Where's he practicing?

All.   In the   dark.

Practicing, practicing, practicing, practicing!

Practicing   English   all the   time!

A. MATCHING OPPOSITES

Write the correct letter in the blank.

_f_	1. tall		a.	thin
_____	2. heavy		b.	ugly
_____	3. handsome		c.	single
_____	4. rich		d.	cheap
_____	5. married		e.	poor
_____	6. easy		f.	short
_____	7. expensive		g.	old
_____	8. young		h.	noisy
_____	9. large		i.	difficult
_____	10. quiet		j.	small

B. WHAT ARE THEY SAYING?

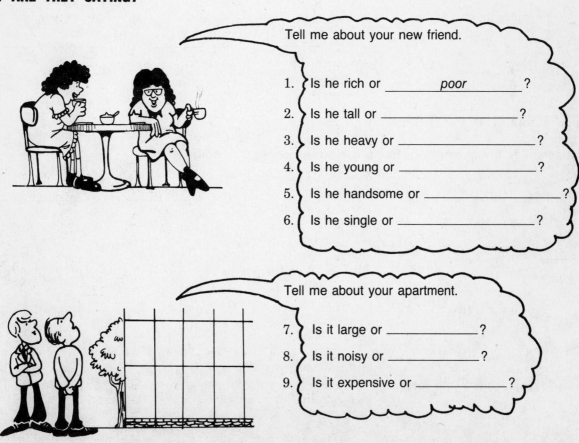

Tell me about your new friend.

1. Is he rich or _____ _poor_ _____?
2. Is he tall or _____?
3. Is he heavy or _____?
4. Is he young or _____?
5. Is he handsome or _____?
6. Is he single or _____?

Tell me about your apartment.

7. Is it large or _____?
8. Is it noisy or _____?
9. Is it expensive or _____?

C. WHAT'S WRONG?

Correct the sentences.

> He ⎫
> She ⎬ isn't   They aren't
> It ⎭

1. He's quiet.

   He isn't quiet.

   He's noisy.

2. It's cheap.

   _____

   _____

3. He's thin.

   _____

   _____

4. She's ugly.

   _____

   _____

5. He's short.

   _____

   _____

6. They're young.

   _____

   _____

D. SCRAMBLED QUESTIONS

Unscramble the questions.   Begin each question with a capital letter.

1. __Is__ __English__ __difficult__ ?
   difficult English is

2. _____ _____ _____?
   tall are you

3. _____ _____ _____?
   they are rich

4. _____ _____ _____
   _____?
   apartment your large is

5. _____ _____ _____?
   I beautiful am

6. _____ _____ _____ _____
   _____?   rich or poor she is

7. _____ _____ _____ _____
   _____?
   neighbors are noisy your

8. _____ _____ _____
   _____ _____?
   John Mary and married are

28

E. RHYTHM AND RHYME: *Old! Cold! Tall! Small!*

Listen.   Then clap and practice.

All.   Is he   young?   (clap) (clap)

Is he   old?   (clap) (clap)

Is it   hot?   (clap) (clap)

Is it   cold?   (clap) (clap)

Is she   short?   (clap) (clap)

Is she   tall?   (clap) (clap)

Is it   large?   (clap) (clap)

Is it   small?   (clap) (clap)

Young!   Old!   Hot!   Cold!

Young!   Old!   Hot!   Cold!

A.   Is he young or   old?

B.   He's very   old.

A.   Is it hot or   cold?

B.   It's very   cold.

A.   Is she short or   tall?

B.   She's very   tall.

A.   Is it large or   small?

B.   It's extremely   small.

All.   Young!   Old!   Hot!   Cold!

Short!   Tall!   Large!   Small!

F. MARGARET'S PHOTOGRAPHS

Label the photographs.

bicycle	cat	house
boss	dog	piano
car	guitar	sink

1. Helen: _____Helen's_____ _____car_____

2. Judy: _____

3. Mr. and Mrs. Pepper: _____ _____ _____

_____ _____

4. Patty: _____

5. Michael: _____

6. John: _____

7. Mr. Sharp: _____ _____ _____

8. Peter: _____

9. Jim: _____

G. WHAT'S THE WORD?

his	their
her	its

(John's)   1. _____His_____ sister is married.

(Judy's)   2. _____ apartment is small.

(Fred and Sally's) 3. _____ dog is noisy.

(Miss Green's)   4. _____ car is new.

(Mr. and Mrs. Brown's) 5. _____ restaurant is cheap.

(Sam's)   6. _____ neighbors are quiet.

(Barbara's)   7. _____ brother is handsome.

(Mr. Larson's)   8. _____ cat is ugly.

(The dog's)   9. _____ name is Fido.

H. MEET FRED McQUEEN

$$\text{Yes,} \begin{cases} \text{I am.} \\ \begin{Bmatrix} \text{he} \\ \text{she} \\ \text{it} \end{Bmatrix} \text{is.} \\ \begin{Bmatrix} \text{we} \\ \text{you} \\ \text{they} \end{Bmatrix} \text{are.} \end{cases}$$

$$\text{No,} \begin{cases} \text{I'm not.} \\ \begin{Bmatrix} \text{he} \\ \text{she} \\ \text{it} \end{Bmatrix} \text{isn't.} \\ \begin{Bmatrix} \text{we} \\ \text{you} \\ \text{they} \end{Bmatrix} \text{aren't.} \end{cases}$$

Fred McQueen is tall and handsome. He isn't fat, and he isn't thin. He's very rich. Fred's car is new and beautiful. His house is large and expensive. His neighbors are rich and quiet. Fred isn't married.

1. Is Fred tall?   _Yes,_ _he_ _is._

2. Is he short?   _____ _____ _____

3. Is he fat?   _____ _____ _____

4. Is he thin?   _____ _____ _____

5. Is he handsome? _____ _____ _____

6. Is he poor?   _____ _____ _____

7. Is Fred's car new? _____ _____ _____

8. Is it ugly?   _____ _____ _____

9. Is his house small? _____ _____ _____

10. Is it cheap?   _____ _____ _____

11. Are his neighbors rich? _____ _____ _____

12. Are they noisy?   _____ _____ _____

13. Is Fred single?   _____ _____ _____

0	zero	10	ten	20	twenty	30	thirty
1	one	11	eleven	21	twenty-one	40	forty
2	two	12	twelve	22	twenty-two	50	fifty
3	three	13	thirteen	23	twenty-three	60	sixty
4	four	14	fourteen	24	twenty-four	70	seventy
5	five	15	fifteen	25	twenty-five	80	eighty
6	six	16	sixteen	26	twenty-six	90	ninety
7	seven	17	seventeen	27	twenty-seven	100	one hundred
8	eight	18	eighteen	28	twenty-eight		
9	nine	19	nineteen	29	twenty-nine		

Listen to the addresses of buildings.   Fill in the correct numbers on the buildings.

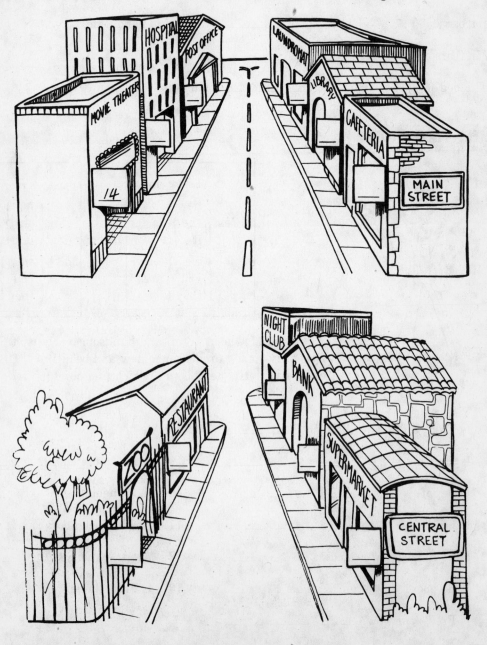

J. THE WEATHER

it's sunny	it's warm	it's cold	it's raining
it's cloudy	it's cool	it's hot	it's snowing

Tokyo   Madrid   London   Boston

San Juan   Mexico City   Hong Kong   Warsaw

1. How's the weather in Tokyo?   _It's_ _____ _sunny._ _____

2. How's the weather in London?   _____ _____

3. How's the weather in Mexico City?   _____ _____

4. How's the weather in Warsaw?   _____ _____

5. How's the weather in Hong Kong?   _____ _____

6. How's the weather in Madrid?   _____ _____

7. How's the weather in San Juan?   _____ _____

8. How's the weather in Boston?   _____ _____

9. How's the weather in your city?   ....

K. LISTEN

Listen to the temperature in Fahrenheit and Celsius.   Write the numbers you hear.

1. Moscow   _34°_ F/ _1°_ C   5. Paris   _____ F/ _____ C

2. Cairo   _____ F/ _____ C   6. Athens   _____ F/ _____ C

3. Caracas   _____ F/ _____ C   7. Tokyo   _____ F/ _____ C

4. San Francisco _____ F/ _____ C   8. Rio de Janeiro _____ F/ _____ C

33

L. RHYTHM AND RHYME: *Terrible Weather! Beautiful Weather!*

Listen.   Then clap and practice.

It's raining in   Alaska.

It's snowing in   L.A.

It's cloudy in   Caracas.

It's TERRIBLE   today!

It's warm in Pennsylvania.

It's sunny in   Bombay.

It's cool in   Guatemala.

It's BEAUTIFUL   today!

M.   RHYTHM AND RHYME: *How's the Weather?*

Listen.   Then clap and practice.

How's the weather in   Chicago in the   summer?

How's the weather in   Seattle in the   fall?

How's the weather in   Miami in the   winter?

How's the weather in the spring in   Montreal?

It's hot in   Chicago in the   summer.

It's cool in   Seattle in the   fall.

It's warm in   Miami in the   winter.

It's lovely in the spring in   Montreal.

A. OUR FAMILY

husband
wife

Ted   Jane

Ted and Jane are married.

1. Ted is Jane's _____*husband*_____ .

2. Jane is Ted's _____ .

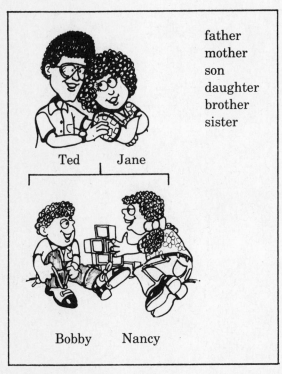

father
mother
son
daughter
brother
sister

Ted   Jane

Bobby   Nancy

grandfather
grandmother
grandson
granddaughter

Fred   Hilda

Ted   Jane

Bobby   Nancy

3. Bobby is Ted and Jane's _____ .

4. Nancy is their _____ .

5. Jane is Bobby and Nancy's

    _____ .

6. Ted is their _____ .

7. Bobby is Nancy's _____ .

8. Nancy is Bobby's _____ .

9. Hilda is Bobby and Nancy's

    _____ .

10. Fred is their _____ .

11. Bobby is Fred and Hilda's

    _____ .

12. Nancy is their _____ .

B. WHERE ARE THEY? WHAT ARE THEY DOING?

sitting	in front of	beach
standing		bench
swimming		

1. They're _____
   on the sofa.

2. He's at the _____ .

3. She's _____ .

4. She's _____ .

5. They're _____
   the fireplace.

6. She's sitting on the

   _____ .

C. OUT OF PLACE

Circle the word that doesn't belong.

1. car: garage, fixing, (cooking,) washing

2. beach: swimming, sink, hot, sunny

3. park: birds, bench, bank, soccer

4. living room: fireplace, television, sink, sofa

5. birthday party: sleeping, singing, dancing, eating

6. family: daughter, mother, neighbor, son

7. apartment: living room, bedroom, kitchen, classroom

8. weather: cloudy, short, raining, cool

9. eating: breakfast, newspaper, lunch, dinner

10. drinking: tea, birds, champagne, coffee

11. playing: guitar, baseball, piano, car

12. Bob: pretty, rich, tall, handsome

13. house: expensive, quiet, fat, beautiful

14. children: young, noisy, small, cloudy

36

D. A LETTER FROM NEW YORK CITY

> *Friday, June 10*
>
> *Dear Walter,*
>
>   *We're on vacation in New York City, and we're having a good time. New York is beautiful. The weather is hot and sunny. It's 80°F.*
>
>   *Today my mother and father are at the Statue of Liberty. My sister, Julie, is swimming at the beach, and my brother, Henry, and his friends are playing soccer in the park.*
>
>   *I'm in Aunt Martha and Uncle Charlie's apartment. It's large and beautiful. Aunt Martha is cooking a big dinner, and Uncle Charlie is singing and playing the guitar.*
>
>   *Cousin Tommy and Cousin Gloria aren't on vacation. They're doing their homework in front of the TV. Their homework isn't easy.*
>
>   *How is the weather in Los Angeles? Is it hot?*
>
>   *What are you and your family doing? Are you studying?*
>
>   *See you soon,*
>   *Cousin Michael*

Answer the questions in complete sentences.

1. How's the weather in New York City?   *It's hot and sunny.* _____

2. What's the temperature in New York? _____

3. Where are Michael's mother and father? _____

4. Who is Julie? _____

5. Where is she? _____

6. What's she doing? _____

7. Who is Henry? _____

8. Where is he? _____

9. What's he doing? _____

10. Where's Michael? _____

11. What's Aunt Martha doing? _____

12. Who is Charlie? _____

13. What's he doing? _____

14. Where are Tommy and Gloria? _____

15. What are they doing? _____

16. Who is Walter? _____

E. STRESS AND RHYME: *No. SHE'S in SPAIN.*

Listen.   Then clap and practice.

A.   What's Jack   doing?

B.   He's working in Rome.

A.   What's BOB   doing?

B.   He's working at HOME.

A.   Is Jack at   home?

B.   No.   HE'S in   ROME.

A.   Is BOB in   Rome?

B.   No.   HE's at   HOME.

All.   Jack's in   Rome.

              Jack's in   Rome.

     What's BOB   doing?

          He's working at HOME.

A.   What's Jane   doing?

B.   She's working in Spain.

A.   What's MARY   doing?

B.   She's working in   MAINE.

A.   Is Jane in   MAINE?

B.   No.   SHE'S in   SPAIN.

A.   Is MARY in   Spain?

B.   No.   SHE'S in   MAINE.

All.   Jane's in   Spain.

              Jane's in   Spain.

     What's MARY   doing?

          She's working in   MAINE.

CHECK-UP TEST: *Chapters 4–6*

A. Put a circle around the correct answer.

Ex. The children are noisy. They're [reading / sleeping / (singing)] .

1. Bob is standing [in / on / at] front of the fireplace.

2. Rita is swimming at the [beach / bench / bank] .

3. Jane is [brushing / painting / washing] her teeth.

4. Peter is doing his [sink / homework / room] .

5. Michael's in the kitchen. He's fixing the [sofa / sink / bed] .

6. Betty is sitting on the [sofa / TV / apartment] .

7. Are you married? Yes, I [is / am / are] .

8. Are your neighbors rich? No, [we / you / they] aren't.

9. The cat is eating [its / it's / he's] dinner.

10. Where's Mr. Smith's car? [His / Her / Its] car is in the garage.

11. Where are Mrs. Johnson's neighbors? [His / Her / Their] neighbors are in the park.

12. Where's Mr. and Mrs. Brown's dog? [Her / His / Their] dog is in the bedroom.

13. [Who / Where / What] is he? He's my father.

14. My mother's mother is my [aunt / sister / grandmother] .

15. Is your house large? No, [their / her / our] house is small.

B. Write a sentence with the opposite adjective.

Ex. My apartment isn't large. ___*It's small.*___

1. Mr. and Mrs. Smith aren't quiet.

   _____

2. My husband isn't ugly. _____

3. We aren't heavy. _____

4. Miss Jones isn't young. _____

5. English isn't difficult. _____

C. Write the question.

Ex. ___*Is she ugly*___ ? No, she isn't. She's beautiful.

1. _____ ? No, it isn't. It's hot.

2. _____ ? No, he isn't. He's short.

3. _____ ? No, I'm not. I'm poor.

4. _____ ? No, they aren't. They're expensive.

5. _____ ? No, we aren't. We're single.

39

7

A. WHERE IS IT?

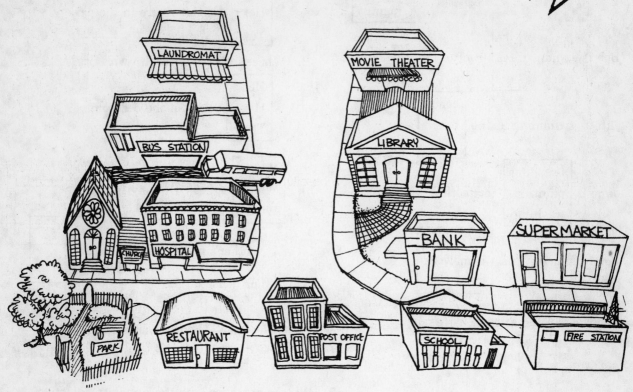

across from	around the corner from	between	next to

1. The park is _____ *next to* _____ the restaurant.

2. The school is _____ the fire station.

3. The fire station is _____ the supermarket.

4. The post office is _____ the restaurant and the school.

5. The bank is _____ the library.

6. The supermarket is _____ the bank.

7. The restaurant is _____ the park and the post office.

8. The laundromat is _____ the movie theater.

9. The church is _____ the hospital.

10. The bus station is _____ the hospital.

B. WHAT ARE THEY SAYING?

Is there?
Yes, there is.
There's _____ .

across from
around the corner from
between
next to

1. Excuse me. Is there a library in this neighborhood?

   Yes, there is. _____*There's*_____ a library on Main Street, _____*across from*_____ the school.

2. Excuse me. _____ a hospital in this neighborhood?

   Yes, there is. _____ a hospital on State Street, _____ the park.

3. Excuse me. Is there a movie theater in this neighborhood?

   Yes, _____ . _____ a movie theater on Central Avenue, _____ the bank.

4. Excuse me. _____ a church nearby?

   Yes, there is. _____ a church on State Street, _____ the library and the _____ .

5. Excuse me. _____ a post office in this neighborhood?

   Yes, _____ . _____ a post office on _____ Street, _____ the laundromat.

41

Listen to these sentences about the buildings on the map.   After each sentence write the name on the correct building.

1. fire station
2. police station
3. gas station
4. train station

5. school
6. drug store
7. church
8. cafeteria

9. restaurant
10. movie theater
11. clinic
12. post office

13. supermarket
14. library

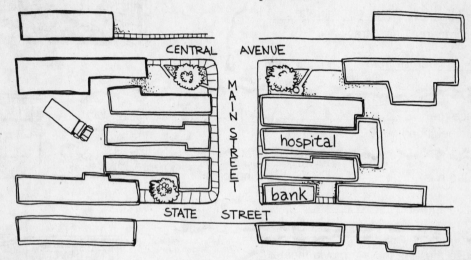

CENTRAL   AVENUE

MAIN STREET

hospital

bank

STATE   STREET

D. **YES OR NO**

Look at the map and answer the questions.

> Yes, there is.
> No, there isn't.

1. Is there a gas station on Main Street? _____ *Yes, there is.* _____

2. Is there a movie theater across from the train station? _____

3. Is there a supermarket around the corner from the drug store? _____

4. Is there a post office across from the library? _____

5. Is there a school between the church and the fire station? _____

6. Is there a bank across from the movie theater? _____

7. Is there a police station next to the bank? _____

8. Is there a restaurant on Central Avenue? _____

9. Is there a hospital between the church and the fire station? _____

10. Is there a church next to the bank? _____

E. RHYTHM: *Where's the Bank?*

Listen. Then clap and practice.

A.   Where's the   bank?

B.   It's next to the drug store.

A.   Where's the   drug store?

B.   It's next to the bank.

A.   Where's the   church?

B.   It's across from the book store.

A.   Where's the   book store?

B.   It's across from the church.

All.   Books in the   book store.

Money in the   bank.

Books in the   book store.

Money in the   bank.

People in the church.

People in the drug store.

Books in the   book store.

Money in the   bank.

F. RHYTHM: *Just Around the Corner*

Listen. Then clap and practice.

All.   There's a nice big   supermarket   just around the   corner.

There's a good cheap   restaurant   just around the   corner.

There's a nice clean   laundromat   just around the   corner.

There's a wonderful   book store   just around the   corner.

There's a quiet little   park   just around the   corner,

just around the   corner,

just around the   corner.

(continued) 43

A. Is there a good supermarket anywhere around here?
B. Yes, there is. Yes, there is.
    There's a nice big supermarket just around the corner.
A. Just around the corner? Thanks very much.

A. Is there a good restaurant anywhere around here?
B. Yes, there is. Yes, there is.
    There's a good cheap restaurant just around the corner.
A. Just around the corner? Thanks very much.

A. Is there a good laundromat anywhere around here?
B. Yes, there is. Yes, there is.
    There's a nice clean laundromat just around the corner.
A. Just around the corner? Thanks very much.

A. Is there a good book store anywhere around here?
B. Yes, there is. Yes, there is.
    There's a wonderful book store just around the corner.
A. Just around the corner? Thanks very much.

A. Is there a nice park anywhere around here?
B. Yes, there is. Yes, there is.
    There's a quiet little park just around the corner.
A. Just around the corner? Thanks very much.

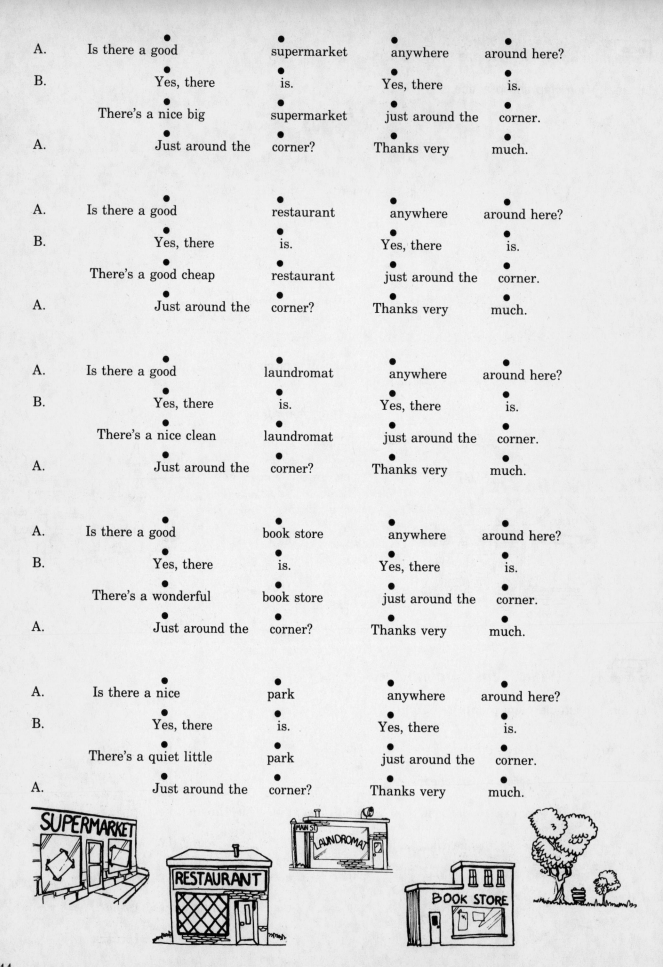

44

G. WHAT ARE THEY SAYING?

1. ___Is___ ___there___ an elevator in the building?

2. Yes, _____ _____.

3. How many closets _____ _____ in the apartment?

4. _____ a large closet in the hallway and _____ _____ two small closets in the bedroom.

5. _____ _____ any windows in the kitchen?

6. No, _____ _____. But _____ a big window in the living room.

H. OUR APARTMENT BUILDING

broken
closet
fire escape
mailbox
mice
pets
radiators
roof
stove
superintendent

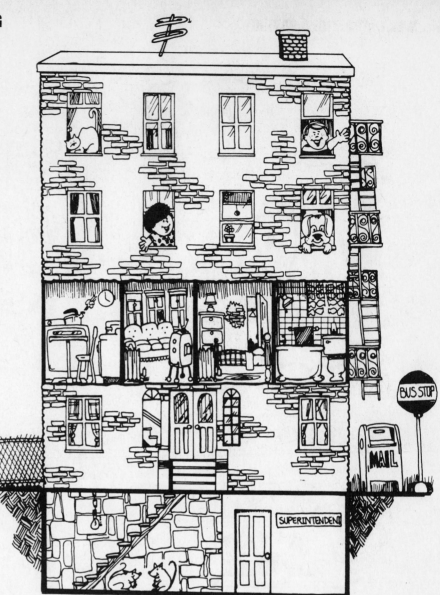

1. There's a TV antenna on the _____ *roof* _____ .

2. There's a _____ in the kitchen across from the sink.

3. There are _____ in the bedroom and living room.   They're hot.

4. There's a _____ next to the bathroom.

5. There are two _____ in the building: a cat and a dog.

6. There aren't any clothes in the _____ in the bedroom.

7. There's a _____ between the building and the bus stop.

8. There are two _____ in the basement.

9. The _____'s apartment is in the basement.

10. There's a _____ window in the living room.

I. BARBARA'S LIVING ROOM

Yes, there is.	Yes, there are.
No, there isn't.	No, there aren't.

1. Is there a TV in Barbara's living room? _____ *Yes, there is.* _____

2. Is there a fireplace in Barbara's living room? _____

3. Are there any windows? _____

4. Are there any books on the TV? _____

5. Are there any clothes in the closet? _____

6. Is there a dog in front of the fireplace? _____

7. Is there a cat in the closet? _____

8. Are there any photographs on the piano? _____

9. Are there any cards on the sofa? _____

10. Are there any pets in Barbara's living room? _____

11. Is there a closet next to the fireplace? _____

(continued)

12. Is there a newspaper in the closet? _____

13. Is there a guitar on the sofa? _____

14. How many books are there on the sofa? _____

15. How many photographs are there on the piano? _____

16. How many pets are there in the room? _____

17. How many cards are there on the piano? _____

18. How many windows are there in the room? _____

J. LOOKING FOR AN APARTMENT

apt. = apartment	dinrm. = dining room	livrm. = living room
bath(s). = bathroom(s)	elev. = elevator	nr. = near
bdrm(s). = bedroom(s)	frpl(s). = fireplace(s)	rm(s). = room(s)
beaut. = beautiful	kit. = kitchen	schl. = school
bldg. = building	lge. = large	

DETROIT, quiet, sunny apt., kit., livrm., bdrm., bath., 2 frpls., nr. bus, no children. $500. 492–5683.

1. The apartment is in _____ *Detroit* _____ .

2. It's quiet and _____ .

3. There's a kitchen, a living room, a _____ , and a _____ .

4. There are two _____ in the apartment.

5. There aren't any _____ in the building.

BOSTON, sunny, lge. apt., kit., livrm., dinrm., 2 bdrms., bath., frpl., nr. schl., no pets. $800. 666–1700.

6. The apartment is in _____ .

7. It's sunny and _____ .

8. There are two _____ in the apartment.

9. _____ a fireplace in the apartment.

10. There's a _____ near the building.

11. There _____ any pets in the building.

LOS ANGELES, beaut. new apt., kit., livrm., 3 bdrms., 2 baths., elev. in bldg. $600. 715–8362.

12. The apartment is in _____ .

13. It's _____ and new.

14. _____ _____ three _____ in the apartment.

15. There's an elevator in the _____ .

48

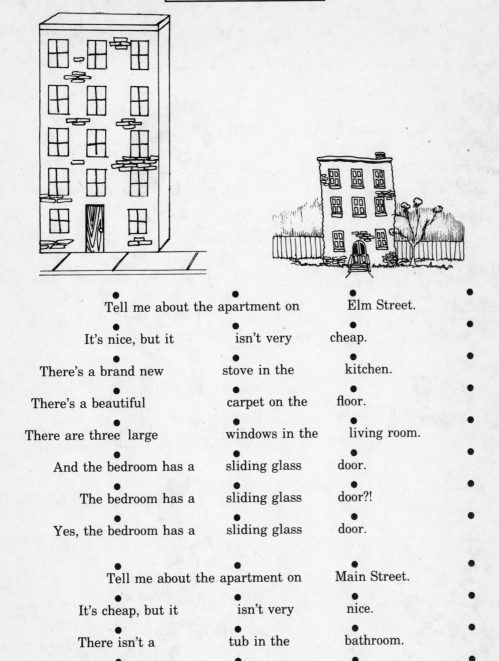

K. RHYTHM AND RHYME: *Tell Me About the Apartment*

Listen.   Then clap and practice.

There are = Thére're

A.   Tell me about the apartment on   Elm Street.

B.   It's nice, but it   isn't very   cheap.

There's a brand new   stove in the   kitchen.

There's a beautiful   carpet on the   floor.

There are three large   windows in the   living room.

And the bedroom has a   sliding glass   door.

All.   The bedroom has a   sliding glass   door?!

B.   Yes, the bedroom has a   sliding glass   door.

A.   Tell me about the apartment on   Main Street.

B.   It's cheap, but it   isn't very   nice.

There isn't a   tub in the   bathroom.

There aren't any   lights in the   hall.

There's a broken   window in the   dining room.

And there are ten big   holes in the   wall!

All.   There are ten big   holes in the   wall?!

B.   Yes, there are ten big   holes in the   wall.

49

A. WHAT ARE THEY WEARING?

belt	coat	jacket	raincoat	stocking
blouse	dress	mitten	shirt	suit
boot	earring	necklace	shoe	sweater
bracelet	glasses	pants	skirt	tie
briefcase	glove	purse	sock	umbrella
	hat			watch

1.   *hat*

2. _____

3. _____

4. _____

5. _____

6. _____

7. _____

8. _____

9. _____

10. _____

11. _____

12. _____

13. _____

14. _____

15. _____

16. _____

17. _____

18. _____

19. _____

20. _____

21. _____

22. _____

23. _____

24. _____

25. _____

26. _____

27. _____

B. A/AN

1. _a_ bank	7. ___ hospital	13. ___ island	19. ___ uncle
2. ___ school	8. ___ antenna	14. ___ house	20. ___ neighbor
3. ___ umbrella	9. ___ elevator	15. ___ apartment	21. ___ hole
4. ___ radio	10. ___ yard	16. ___ library	22. ___ earring
5. ___ office	11. ___ beach	17. ___ window	23. ___ woman
6. ___ post office	12. ___ airport	18. ___ aunt	24. ___ exercise

C. SINGULAR/PLURAL

1. a hat / _hats_

2. _a_ _glove_ / gloves

3. _____ _____ / sweaters

4. a necklace / _____

5. a tie / _____

6. a dress / _____

7. _____ _____ / classes

8. a watch / _____

9. _____ _____ / beaches

10. a bench / _____

11. a church / _____

12. an exercise / _____

13. _____ _____ / men

14. a woman / _____

15. _____ _____ / children

16. a mouse / _____

17. _____ _____ / teeth

18. _____ _____ / people

51

D. LISTEN

Listen to each word.   Put a circle around the word you hear.

1. coat   (coats)   9. necklace   necklaces

2. car   cars   10. earring   earrings

3. umbrella   umbrellas   11. belt   belts

4. exercise   exercises   12. watch   watches

5. dog   dogs   13. bank   banks

6. shoe   shoes   14. house   houses

7. dress   dresses   15. jacket   jackets

8. restaurant restaurants   16. glove   gloves

E. COLORS

Write sentences about yourself, using colors.

red	orange	yellow	green	blue	purple
black	brown	pink	gray	white	gold
silver					

1. My house/apartment is ....

2. My bedroom is ....

3. My kitchen is ....

4. My classroom is ....

5. My English book is ....

6. My shoes are ....

7. My socks/stockings are ....

8. My coat is ....

9. My hat is ....

10. My teeth are ....

11. My classroom is ....

12. My .... (is/are) ....

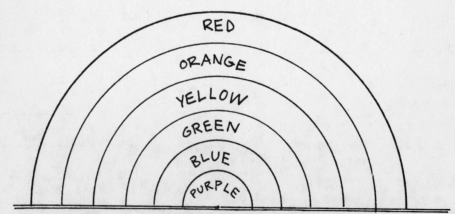

F. WHAT'S IN MR. AND MRS. JACKSON'S CLOSET?

a _____ a pair of _____ two _____

a _____ a pair of _____ two _____

a _____ a pair of _____ three _____

an _____ a pair of _____ three _____

a pair of _____ four _____

a pair of _____

a pair of _____

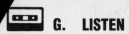
Listen to each sentence. Put a check (✔) next to the appropriate picture.

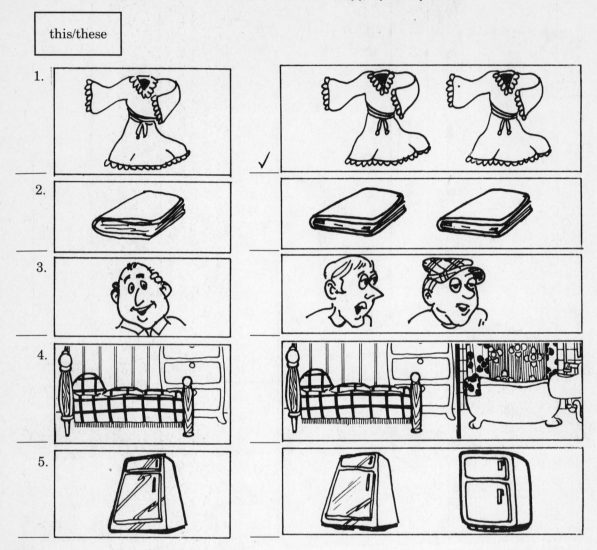

this/these

H. LISTEN

Listen and circle the correct word to complete the sentence.

1. (is) / are red.   5. is / are beautiful.

2. is / are easy.   6. is / are gold.

3. is / are big.   7. is / are expensive.

4. is / are green.   8. is / are white.

I. THIS / THAT / THESE / THOSE

blue

red

1. _____ *This book is blue.* _____

2. _____ *That book is red.* _____

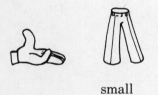

gold

silver

3. _____

4. _____

green

purple

5. _____

6. _____

small

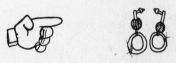

big

7. _____

8. _____

cheap

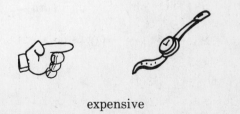

expensive

9. _____

10. _____

55

J. SINGULAR→PLURAL

Write the sentences in the plural.

1. This hat is red. _____*These hats are red.*_____

2. That skirt is short. _____

3. This watch is gold. _____

4. This necklace isn't expensive. _____

5. That dress is beautiful. _____

6. This woman is rich. _____

7. This is my child. _____

8. That isn't your pencil. _____

9. Is that your glove? _____

10. This isn't my sock. _____

K. PLURAL→SINGULAR

Write the sentences in the singular.

1. These bracelets are silver. _____*This bracelet is silver.*_____

2. Those exercises are easy. _____

3. Are these your friends? _____

4. Are those your books? _____

5. These are Sally's blouses. _____

6. These men are my neighbors. _____

7. These aren't my mittens. _____

8. Those aren't my shoes. _____

9. Those churches are nearby. _____

10. Those are George's pets. _____

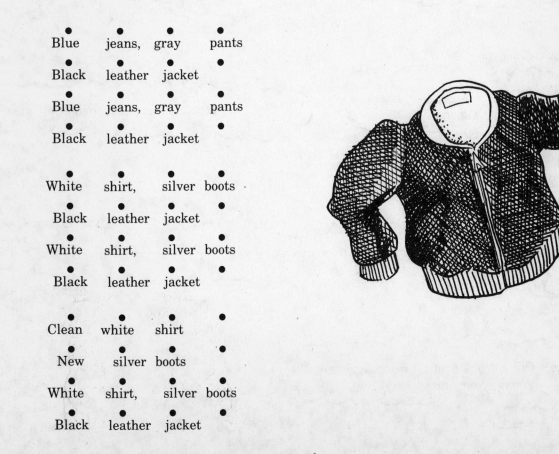

L. RHYTHM AND RHYME: *Clothes in My Closet*

Listen. Then clap and practice.

This shirt is red.
That skirt is blue.
This shirt is old.
That skirt is new.

Old red shirt!
New blue skirt!
Old red shirt!
New blue skirt!

These suits are silver.
Those boots are gold.
These suits are new.
Those boots are old.

New silver suits!
Old gold boots!
New silver suits!
Old gold boots!

M. RHYTHM: *Black Leather Jacket*

Listen. Then clap and practice.

Blue jeans, gray pants
Black leather jacket
Blue jeans, gray pants
Black leather jacket

White shirt, silver boots
Black leather jacket
White shirt, silver boots
Black leather jacket

Clean white shirt
New silver boots
White shirt, silver boots
Black leather jacket

57

N. ALICE'S PHOTOGRAPH

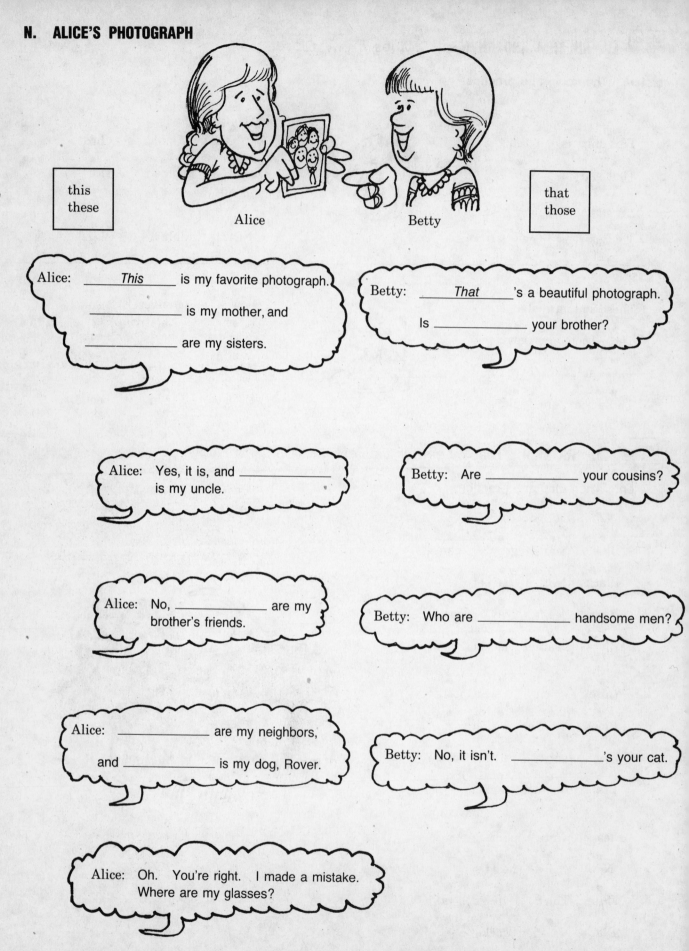

this
these

Alice   Betty

that
those

Alice: _____This_____ is my favorite photograph.

_____ is my mother, and

_____ are my sisters.

Betty: _____That_____'s a beautiful photograph.

Is _____ your brother?

Alice: Yes, it is, and _____ is my uncle.

Betty: Are _____ your cousins?

Alice: No, _____ are my brother's friends.

Betty: Who are _____ handsome men?

Alice: _____ are my neighbors, and _____ is my dog, Rover.

Betty: No, it isn't. _____'s your cat.

Alice: Oh. You're right. I made a mistake. Where are my glasses?

CHECK-UP TEST: *Chapters 7–8*

A. Put a circle around the correct answer.

Ex. My teeth are
- red
- (white)
- blue

1. Jane is wearing a pair of
   - dresses
   - blouses
   - pants

2. This
   - questions
   - homework
   - exercises

   is easy.

3.
   - These
   - They
   - There's

   a church next to the bank.

4. Is there a shirt on the bed?
   No,
   - they isn't
   - there isn't
   - there aren't

5.
   - What
   - Who
   - How

   many rooms are there in the house?

6. There's a
   - woman
   - umbrella
   - earring

   on the sofa.

7. There aren't any
   - window
   - pet
   - children

   in the building.

B. Put a circle around the word that doesn't belong.

Ex. this, (their,) those, that, these

1. green, yellow, silver, glove, gray

2. blouse, shirt, sweater, coat, briefcase

3. church, drug store, fire escape, school, laundromat

4. sister, brother, mother, house, father

C. Answer the questions.

Ex. Where's the post office?

It's around the corner from the hospital.

1. Where's the restaurant?

2. Where's the school?

3. Where's the supermarket?

(continued)

D. Write sentences with *this, that, these,* and *those.*

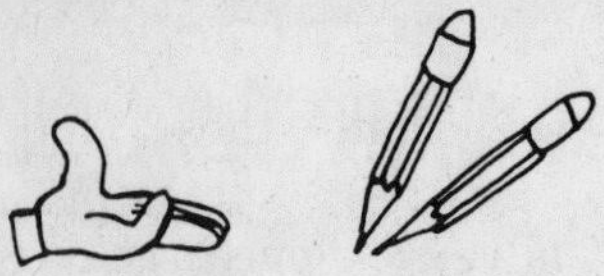

yellow

Ex.   *These pencils are yellow.*

blue

1. _____

brown

2. _____

expensive

3. _____

E. Write the sentences in the plural.

Ex. This exercise is easy.

        These exercises are easy.

1. This dress is beautiful.

    _____

2. That isn't my pen.

_____

3. Is that your briefcase?

_____

4. This watch isn't gold.

_____

F. Listen to the beginning of each sentence. Circle the correct word to complete the sentence.

Ex. | is
(are) | white.

1. | is
are | beautiful.

2. | is
are | green.

3. | is
are | new.

4. | is
are | red.

A. INTERVIEWS AROUND THE WORLD

9

what	language	we	our	is	drink	read
what's	name	you	your	are	eat	sing
where	names	they	their	do	live	speak

1. _____What's_____ your name?

2. My _____ _____ Mario.

3. Where _____ _____ live?

4. I _____ in Rome.

5. _____ _____ do you speak?

6. I _____ Italian.

7. What _____ _____ do every day?

8. Every day I _____ Italian food and I _____ Italian songs.

9. What _____ your names?

10. _____ _____ are Sara and Mark.

11. Where do _____ _____?

12. _____ _____ in London.

13. _____ language _____ _____ speak?

14. We _____ English.

15. What _____ you _____ every day?

16. Every day _____ _____ English tea and we _____ English newspapers.

61

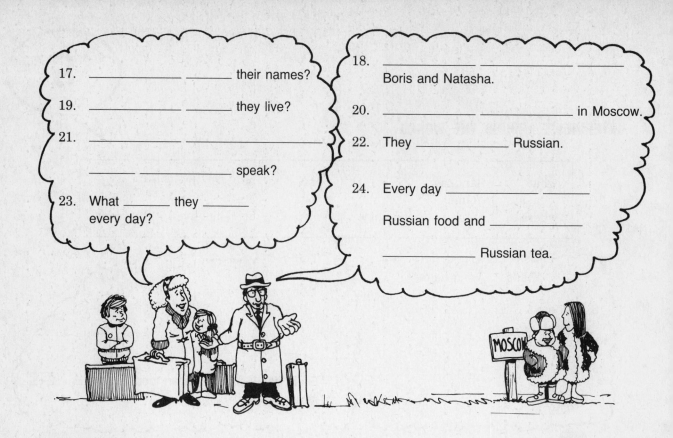

17. _____ _____ their names?

19. _____ _____ they live?

21. _____ _____

_____ _____ speak?

23. What _____ they _____ every day?

18. _____ _____ _____ Boris and Natasha.

20. _____ _____ in Moscow.

22. They _____ Russian.

24. Every day _____ _____ Russian food and _____ _____ Russian tea.

B. PEOPLE AROUND THE WORLD

1. What's his name? _____ *His name is Frank.* _____

2. Where does he live? _____

3. What does he do every day? _____

62

4. _____? His name is Robert.

5. _____? He lives in Paris.

6. What language does he speak? _____

7. What _____ every day? He _____ French books _____

_____.

8. What's her name? _____

9. _____ she live? _____

10. What language _____? She _____.

11. _____ every day? She _____

_____.

C. WRITE ABOUT YOURSELF

1. What's your name? ....

2. Where do you live? ....

3. What language do you speak? ....

4. What do you do every day? ....

....

D. RHYTHM AND RHYME: *People and Places*

Listen. Then clap and practice.

A. What's his   name?
B. His name is   Joe.
A. Where does he live?
B. In Mexico.

A. What's his   name?
B. His name is   Lance.
A. Where does he live?
B. He lives in   France.

A. What's her   name?
B. Her name is   Anne.
A. Where does she live?
B. She lives in   Japan.

A. What's her   name?
B. Her name is Anastasia.
A. Where does she live?
B. She lives in   Malaysia.

A. What's her   name?
B. Her name is   Denise.
A. Where does she live?
B. She lives in   Greece.

A. What's her   name?
B. Her name is   Maria.
A. Where does she live?
B. She lives in   Korea.

E. MARIA'S FAMILY

Put a circle around the correct word.

(1) My name is Maria. (2) I [**live**] / lives in London. (3) I [speak / speaks] English and Spanish. (4) My husband's name is John. (5) He [speak / speaks] English.

(6) Our children, Fred and Sara, [speak / speaks] English and Spanish. (7) At school they [sing / sings] English and Spanish songs.

(8) We [live / lives] in a big house. (9) Every day I [cook / cooks] lunch and dinner, and I [clean / cleans] the house. (10) Every day my husband [cook / cooks] breakfast, and he [clean / cleans] the yard. (11) We [eat / eats] big English breakfasts and big Spanish dinners.

(12) Every day my husband and I [read / reads] the newspaper. (13) We [drink / drinks] tea and we [listen / listens] to the radio. (14) I [read / reads] Spanish newspapers and my husband [read / reads] English newspapers.

(15) What do you [do / does] every day? (16) What languages [do / does] you speak?

F. WRITE ABOUT MARIA'S FAMILY

1. Where does Maria live? _____ *She lives in London.*

2. What languages does she speak? _____

3. What language does Maria's husband speak? _____

4. What languages do Fred and Sara speak? _____

5. What do they do at school? _____

6. What does Maria do every day? _____

   _____

   _____

7. What does John do every day? _____

   _____

   _____

G. LISTEN

Listen to the story.   Write the missing words.

Every day I sit in the park.   I _____ the newspaper, I _____ cards, I
                                        1   2

_____ my lunch, and I _____ to the radio.   _____ not a busy person.
      3   4   5

My friend Harry _____ around the corner from my house.   Every day Harry
                        6

_____ his apartment, he _____ the piano, he _____ books, he
      7   8   9

_____ exercises, and he _____.   My friend Harry _____ a very busy person.
      10   11   12

H. LISTEN AND PRONOUNCE

Listen to each word and then say it.

1. beach	5. Chinese	9. watching	13. she's	17. washing
2. bench	6. church	10. English	14. shirt	18. Washington
3. Charlie	7. kitchen	11. Natasha	15. shoes	
4. children	8. teacher	12. Sharp	16. station	

I. LOUD AND CLEAR

Fill in the words.   Then read the sentences aloud.

beach	Charlie	Chinese

1. _____*Charlie*_____ is eating _____*Chinese*_____

food at the _____*beach*_____ .

Natasha	station	Washington

2. _____ is at the train _____

in _____, D.C.

children	kitchen	watching

3. The _____ are _____ TV

in the _____ .

Sharp	shirt	washing

4. Mr. _____ is _____

a _____ .

bench	church	teacher

5. Our _____ is sitting on a _____

in front of the _____ .

English	she's	shoes

6. _____ wearing an _____ coat

and English _____ .

67

10

MONDAY - RUSSIAN
TUESDAY - JAPANESE
WEDNESDAY - MEXICAN
THURSDAY - ITALIAN
FRIDAY - FRENCH
SATURDAY - GREEK
SUNDAY - GERMAN

Franklin's International Night Club is a very special place. Every day there's a different kind of music. John Franklin plays the piano, and Mary Franklin sings. On Monday John Franklin plays Russian music, and Mary Franklin sings Russian songs.

1. What kind of music does John Franklin play on Tuesday?

On Tuesday he plays
Japanese music.

2. What kind of songs does Mary Franklin sing on Tuesday?

_____
_____

3. What kind of music does John Franklin play on Wednesday?

_____
_____

4. What kind of songs does Mary Franklin sing on Thursday?

_____
_____

5. _____
_____

On Friday she sings French songs.

6. _____
_____

On Saturday he plays Greek music.

7. Does Mary Franklin sing Mexican songs on Wednesday?

Yes, she does.

8. Does John Franklin play Greek music on Thursday?

_____

9. _____ on Sunday?

Yes, he does.

10. _____ on Saturday?

No, she doesn't.

11. _____ on Monday?

Yes, she does.

12. When does John Franklin play Mexican music?

He plays Mexican music on Wednesday.

13. When does Mary Franklin sing French songs?

_____

14. When does Mary Franklin sing Japanese songs?

_____

15. When _____ Italian music?

_____

16. When _____ Greek music?

_____

17. When _____ Mexican songs?

_____

69

B. WHAT'S THE WORD?

> do/does

1. What kind of books ___do___ you read?

2. _____ Margarita like American TV?

3. Why _____ Marie live in Tokyo?

4. Where _____ Mr. and Mrs. Smith play cards?

5. Why _____ Mrs. Wilson clean her house every day?

6. What _____ Mr. Wilson do every day?

7. _____ you like your new school?   Yes, we _____ .

8. When _____ Henry do his homework?

9. What kind of music _____ your mother and father listen to?

10. How many languages _____ you speak?

11. What kind of songs _____ you and your friends sing?

12.

_____ Tommy cry at the doctor's office?

Yes, he _____ .

C. LISTEN

Listen to each question.   Put a circle around the correct answer.

1. a. Mexican music.
   b. American food.
   c. Every day.

2. a. On Monday, Wednesday, and Friday.
   b. At school.
   c. Because they live in London.

3. a. Yes, he does.
   b. No, we don't.
   c. Yes, they do.

4. a. On Tuesday.
   b. We don't go there on Sunday.
   c. Because we like the clothes there.

5. a. He reads the newspaper.
   b. She plays cards.
   c. They feed the birds.

6. a. On Sunday.
   b. In Hong Kong.
   c. Because they like Chinese food.

7. a. On Friday.
   b. Across the street from the supermarket.
   c. Because she's rich.

8. a. He eats lunch.
   b. They play.
   c. Because it's hot.

9. a. No, she doesn't.
   b. No, we don't.
   c. Yes, they do.

10. a. He goes to the supermarket on Monday.
    b. We go to the supermarket on Tuesday.
    c. On Main Street.

D. YES AND NO

YES!

1. My grandfather drinks tea.

2. David and Tommy play baseball.

3. David's sister plays the guitar.

4. Albert and Walter drink lemonade.

5. Walter's father cleans the yard.

6. On Sunday we _____ to church.

7. Mr. and Mrs. Johnson _____ the newspaper.

8. Their children _____ TV.

9. The dog sleeps in the yard.

10. Peter's cat _____ mice.

11. I wear mittens to school.

12. My mother _____ stockings.

13. My sister feeds the dog.

14. On Saturday Mr. Johnson _____ to the beach.

15. Toshi speaks Japanese.

16. Margarita's cousin _____ in New York.

NO!

1. He ___doesn't___ ___drink___ coffee.

2. They _____ _____ soccer.

3. She _____ _____ the piano.

4. They _____ _____ tea.

5. He _____ _____ the apartment.

6. We don't go to school.

7. They don't read books.

8. They don't like homework.

9. It _____ _____ in the house.

10. It doesn't like children.

11. I _____ _____ gloves.

12. She doesn't wear socks.

13. She _____ _____ the cat.

14. He doesn't go to the library.

15. He _____ _____ Greek.

16. He doesn't live in San Juan.

E. WRITE ABOUT YOURSELF

YES!

1. I like ....

2. I play ....

3. I speak ....

4. I eat ....

5. I drink ....

NO!

1. I don't like ....

2. I don't play ....

3. I don't speak ....

4. I don't eat ....

5. I don't drink ....

F. PRONUNCIATION: *They Do, They Don't*

Listen. Then clap and practice.

Does ~~he~~ = Dóesee	Yes ~~he~~ = Yésee	No ~~he~~ = Nóee

A.   Does he eat French   bread?

B.   Yes, he   does.

A.   Does she like Swiss   cheese?

B.   Yes, she   does.

A.   Does he read the   paper?

B.   No, he   doesn't.

A.   Does she watch   TV?

B.   No, she   doesn't.

A.   Do they drink Greek   wine?

B.   Yes, they   do.

A.   Do they speak   Chinese?

B.   Yes, they   do.

A.   Do they go to   movies?

B.   No, they   don't.

A.   Do they drink iced   tea?

B.   No, they   don't.

All.   He eats French bread.

She likes Swiss cheese.

They drink Greek   wine.

And they speak   Chinese.

All.   He doesn't read the paper.

She doesn't watch   TV.

They don't go to   movies.

And they don't drink   tea.

G. A LETTER TO A PEN PAL   Read and practice.

> *Friday*
>
> *Dear Paul,*
>
> *My family and I live in Athens.   We speak Greek.   My mother is a music teacher.   She plays the piano and sings.   My father cooks at a restaurant.*
>
> *My sister Helen and I go to a school near our house.   We study history, Greek, science, mathematics, and English.   My favorite school subject is history.   I don't like mathematics and science, but I like languages.*
>
> *Do you like sports?   Every day at school I play soccer.   On Saturday I play tennis.   Which sports do you play?*
>
> *What kind of music do you like?   I think classical music is beautiful.   I like jazz, but I don't like rock music.*
>
> *What kind of movies do you like?   I like American westerns and Italian comedies.   I think science fiction movies are terrible.*
>
> *Tell me about your family and your school.*
>
> *Your friend,*
> *Anna*

H. YOUR LETTER TO A PEN PAL

English history mathematics music science

baseball football golf hockey soccer tennis

cartoons comedies dramas science fiction westerns

classical music jazz popular music rock music

Dear ....,

My family and I live in ....   We speak

....

At school I study .... , ... , and

....   My favorite subject is ....

I don't like ....

Which sports do you like?   I play .... and

....   I think .... is wonderful.   I don't

like ....

What kind of movies do you like?   I like ....

very much, but I don't like ....

My favorite kind of music is .... , and I

like ....   I don't listen to ....

Tell me about your school and your city.

Your friend,

....

CHECK-UP TEST: *Chapters 9–10*

A. Put a circle around the correct answer.

Ex. I ⬚(like)/likes Japanese cars.

1. Mr. Jones ⬚feed/feeds the dog.

2. John and Mary ⬚don't/doesn't read at home.

3. Where ⬚do/does your sister live?

4. Mrs. Harris and her daughter ⬚play/plays baseball.

5. We ⬚drink/drinks Colombian coffee.

6. How many languages ⬚do/does Bob speak?

B. Fill in the blanks.

Ex. _____What_____ is your name?

1. _____ do you live?

2. _____ kind of music do they like?

3. _____ does Paul go to the bank?
   On Friday.

4. _____ do you listen to the radio every day?
   Because we like music.

5. _____ Frank go to church on Sunday?
   Yes, he _____.

6. _____ does Mrs. Smith do on Tuesday?

C. Fill in the blanks.

Mrs. Williams _____ in Miami.
1

She's old, but she _____ exercises every
2

day. On Monday she _____ her
3

apartment, on Wednesday she _____
4

cards, on Friday she _____ to music,
5

and on Sunday she _____ the
6

newspaper. She doesn't cook dinner on

Sunday because she and her friends _____
7

to Stanley's International Restaurant.

🔲 D. LISTEN

Listen to each question. Put a circle around the correct answer.

Ex. a. French food.
   (b.) Italian songs.
   c. At the night club.

1. a. Yes, she does.
   b. No, they don't.
   c. Because they're young.

2. a. He feeds the birds.
   b. Because it's hot.
   c. On Sunday.

3. a. We study English.
   b. Every day.
   c. Yes, I do.

4. a. They like American music.
   b. He lives on Central Street.
   c. They live on Main Street.

5. a. On Saturday.
   b. Because we like the food.
   c. In Rome.

A. WHAT ARE THEY SAYING?

me	us
him	you
her	them
it	

11

1. Do you like me? — Of course I like *you*.

2. Do you like Bob? — Of course I like _____.

3. Do you like my new tie? — Of course I like _____.

4. Do you like Fred and Martha? — Of course I like _____.

5. Do you like Mary? — Of course I like _____.

6. Does Mary like you? — Of course she likes _____.

7. Does the teacher like you? — Of course he likes _____.

8. Do you like night clubs? — Of course I like _____.

9. Do you like your new apartment?

Of course I like _____.

10. Do you like your new neighbors?

Of course I like _____.

B. WRITE ABOUT YOURSELF

always	usually	sometimes	rarely	never

1. I ....*always*........... read the newspaper.

2. I .... eat breakfast.

3. I .... cook dinner.

4. I .... dance at parties.

5. I .... watch TV.

6. I .... do my homework.

7. I .... listen to American music.

8. I .... go to Italian restaurants.

9. I .... drink champagne at parties.

10. I always ....

11. I usually ....

12. I sometimes ....

13. I rarely ....

14. I never ....

C. WRITE AND SAY IT

Correct the word in parentheses and then say the sentence.

1. John never (feed) ____*feeds*____ his cat.

2. Nancy rarely (help) _____ her brother.

3. Judy always (fix) _____ her car.

4. Mrs. Smith rarely (talk) _____ to her husband.

5. Mary usually (brush) _____ her teeth.

6. My father sometimes (wash) _____ the clothes.

7. Linda never (go) _____ to school.

8. Tommy sometimes (dance) _____ with his sister.

9. Jane usually (study) _____ during the weekend.

10. My grandfather always (sit) _____ on the sofa and (watch) _____ game shows on TV.

Listen.   Then clap and practice.

A.   • I always come to   • English class.
     • I usually come by   • eight.
     • I sometimes get there   early.
     • I never come in   • late.
     • No, I never come in   • late.

All.   • She always comes to   • English class.
       • She usually comes by   • eight.
       • She sometimes gets there   early.
       • She rarely comes in   • late.

A.   • No!   I NEVER come in   • late!

All.   • Oh!   She never comes in   • late!
       • No!   She never comes in   late!

E. WHAT'S THE WORD?

it	her	him	them

1. I always talk to ___*her*___ .

2. Why don't you listen to _____ ?

3. I read _____ on Sunday.

4. I dance with _____ when I go to parties.

5. What do you feed _____ ?

6. Do you wash _____ every day?

F. LISTEN

Listen to each sentence. Put a check (✔) next to the appropriate picture.

G. WHAT ARE THEY SAYING?

have	do	don't
has	does	doesn't

1. _____Does_____ Johnny _____have_____ any brothers?

No. He _____doesn't_____ _____have_____ any brothers, but he _____has_____ a big sister.

2. Do you have any French wine?

No. We _____ _____ any French wine, but we _____ Italian wine.

3. We're looking for our child. She _____ long brown hair.

What color eyes does she _____?

4. Do your children have a good teacher?

Yes. They _____ a wonderful teacher.

5. What kind of car _____ your brother _____?

He _____ a Toyota.

6. _____ they _____ any shirts?

No. They _____ any shirts, but they _____ beautiful ties.

7. _____ your new apartment _____ a dining room?

Yes. It _____ a dining room and a big kitchen.

79

H. LISTEN: *My Grandmother*

Listen to the story.   Write the missing words.

My grandmother *has* brown eyes and gray curly _____*hair*_____.   She's short and
                 1   2
heavy.   She _____ with _____, and I'm very glad.   Here's why I _____
            3   4   5
she's wonderful.

When we _____ to parties, my grandmother always _____ with me.   When I
          6   7
_____ to her, she always _____ to me, and when my friends talk to
       8   9
_____ , she listens to _____ .
  10   11

When I have difficult homework, my grandmother usually _____ me.   When
                                                              12
I'm hungry, she always _____ _____.   When we _____ together, she
                          13   14   15
_____ _____ to me, and when I'm upset, she always _____ with _____ .
  16   17   18   19
My grandmother is rarely upset.   When our clothes are dirty, she _____
                                                                        20
them.   When the sink is broken, she _____ it.   When my little sisters are noisy,
                                          21
she _____ with _____ .   My grandmother is really wonderful.
       22   23

I. YES OR NO

Yes, she is.	No, she isn't.
Yes, she does.	No, she doesn't.

1. Does my grandmother have brown eyes?   _____*Yes, she does.*_____

2. Does she have brown hair?   _____

3. Is she tall?   _____

4. Is she heavy?   _____

5. Does she dance with me when we go to
    parties?   _____

6. Does she watch TV when we eat together?   _____

7. Is she usually upset?   _____

8. Does she listen to my friends when they talk
    to her?   _____

9. Is she noisy?   _____

10. Is she wonderful?   _____

J. A WONDERFUL PERSON

Write five sentences about a person you think is wonderful.   Tell why.

1. ....

2. ....

3. ....

4. ....

5. ....

K. WHAT'S THE WORD?

Put a circle around the correct word.

1. Maria is listening (to) / at / with the radio.

2. My uncle always dances to / at / with me.

3. John is playing soccer to / at / with us.

4. My children never talk to / at / on me.

5. Do you live in / on / at Tokyo?

6. Tell me to / at / about your city.

7. The post office is in / on / between Main Street.

8. I always listen at / to / on the radio when I eat breakfast.

9. I'm having a wonderful time in / on / at my party.

10. Is there a refrigerator in / on / at the kitchen?

11. Do Paul and Robert go to / at / in school?

12. We're looking from / for / to a yellow umbrella.

13. The children are to / at / in the beach.

14. Natasha is wearing a pair of / from / for boots.

15. Alice is sitting in / on / with a bench in / on / with the park.

16. Martha goes to / at / in church in / on / at Sunday.

81

A. WHAT'S THE WORD?

angry	hot	sad
embarrassed	hungry	sick
happy	nervous	thirsty
		tired

1. Henry is wearing a suit at the beach.

   He's _____*hot*_____ .

2. Alice is yawning.   She's _____ .

3. Mr. Smith's students never do their

   homework.   Mr. Smith is _____ .

4. Robert made a mistake in class.

   He's _____ .

5. Gloria likes her new apartment.

   She's _____ .

6. Edward is drinking lemonade.

   He's _____ .

7. Walter's new car is broken.

   He's _____ .

8. Jane has an English test on Monday.

   She's _____ .

9. Paul is eating a big breakfast.

   He's _____ .

10. Peter is in the hospital.

    He's _____ .

B. TELL ME WHY

1. Why is she smiling?

   ___*She's smiling because she's*___ happy.

   She always ___*smiles when she's happy*___ .

2. Why are you yawning?

   _____ tired.

   I always _____ .

3. Why are they shouting?

   _____ angry.

   They always _____ .

4. Why are you shivering?

   _____ cold.

   We always _____ .

5. Why is he perspiring?

   _____ hot.

   He always _____ .

6. Why are they crying?

   _____ sad.

   They always _____ .

7. Why is he going to a restaurant?

   _____ hungry.

   He always _____ .

8. Why is he biting his nails?

   _____ nervous.

   He always _____ .

9.

Why are you blushing?

_____ embarrassed.

I always _____ .

C. RHYTHM AND RHYME: *I Smile When I'm Happy*

Listen. Then clap and practice.

A. I smile when I'm happy.

I frown when I'm sad.

I blush when I'm embarrassed.

And I shout when I'm mad.

B. Are you smiling?

A. Yes. I'm happy.

B. Are you frowning?

A. Yes. I'm sad.

B. Are you blushing?

A. Yes. I'm embarrassed.

B. Are you shouting?

A. Yes. I'm mad.

D. RHYTHM: *Why Are You Doing That?*

Listen. Then clap and practice.

A. What's Fran doing?

B. She's working late.

A. Working late?

Why's she doing that?

B. It's Monday.

She always works late on Monday.

A. What are you doing?

B. We're playing cards.

A. Playing cards?

Why are you doing that?

B. It's Tuesday.

We always play cards on Tuesday.

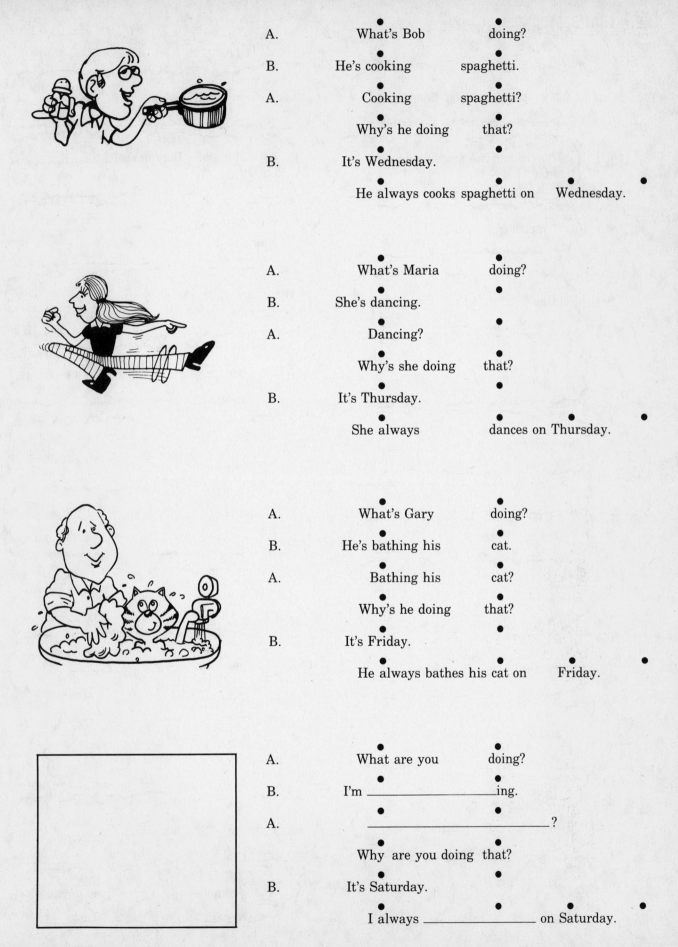

A. What's Bob   doing?

B. He's cooking   spaghetti.

A. Cooking   spaghetti?

    Why's he doing   that?

B. It's Wednesday.

    He always cooks spaghetti on   Wednesday.

A. What's Maria   doing?

B. She's dancing.

A. Dancing?

    Why's she doing   that?

B. It's Thursday.

    She always   dances on Thursday.

A. What's Gary   doing?

B. He's bathing his   cat.

A. Bathing his   cat?

    Why's he doing   that?

B. It's Friday.

    He always bathes his cat on   Friday.

A. What are you   doing?

B. I'm _____ing.

A. _____?

    Why are you doing that?

B. It's Saturday.

    I always _____ on Saturday.

85

E. THAT'S STRANGE!

1. My sister is cooking dinner today.

   That's strange! She never _____cooks_____ dinner.

2. The children are studying English today.

   That's strange! They never _____ English.

3. I'm cleaning my room today.

   That's strange! You never _____ your room.

4. David is playing with his brother.

   That's strange! He never _____ with his brother.

5. The cat _____ _____ in the garage today.

   That's strange! It never sleeps in the garage.

6. Mr. and Mrs. Wilson _____ _____.

   That's strange! They never dance.

7. Our mother _____ _____ the dishes today.

   That's strange! She never _____ the dishes.

8. Our teacher _____ _____ today.

   That's strange! She never smiles.

9. We're watching TV today.

   That's strange. You never _____ TV.

10. Mr. and Mrs. Jones _____ _____ the newspaper today.

    That's strange! They never read the newspaper.

11. Sally is helping her sisters today.

    That's strange! She never _____ them.

12. My brother and I _____ _____ football today.

    That's strange! You never play football.

13. My mother and father are shouting.

That's strange! They never _____.

14. I'm _____ coffee today.

That's strange! You never drink coffee.

15. My grandfather is listening to rock music.

That's strange! He never _____ to rock music.

F. WHAT'S THE QUESTION?

1. I'm crying <u>because I'm sad.</u>   (Why?)   _____*Why are you crying?*_____

2. They play tennis <u>in the park.</u>   (Where?)   _____*Where do they play tennis?*_____

3. She goes to the library <u>on Wednesday.</u>   (When?)   _____

   _____

4. They're singing <u>because they're happy.</u>   (Why?)   _____

5. She's going <u>to the beach.</u>   (Where?)   _____

6. He washes his clothes <u>at the laundromat.</u>   (Where?)   _____

   _____

7. I like <u>Colombian</u> coffee.   (What kind of?)   _____

8. She has <u>ten</u> grandchildren.   (How many?)   _____

9. He's eating <u>at the cafeteria</u> today.   (Where?)   _____

10. I'm wearing <u>two</u> sweaters.   (How many?)   _____

11. She's <u>reading.</u>   (What?)   _____

12. They play <u>soccer</u> on Tuesday.   (What?)   _____

13. He watches <u>game</u> shows.   (What kind of?)   _____

   _____

14. We're cooking a big dinner <u>because we're hungry.</u>   (Why?)   _____

   _____

G. LISTEN

As you listen to each story, read the following sentences and check <u>yes</u> or <u>no</u>.   You will hear each story twice.

      <u>JANE AND BETTY</u>

1. yes ☐   no ☐   Jane and Betty are looking for a laundromat.

2. yes ☐   no ☐   Jane and Betty are very angry.

3. yes ☐   no ☐   Their mother isn't cooking dinner today.

      <u>JACK</u>

4. yes ☐   no ☐   Jack always does his homework.

5. yes ☐   no ☐   He rarely helps his parents in the kitchen.

6. yes ☐   no ☐   His parents are never angry at him.

      <u>TOM</u>

7. yes ☐   no ☐   Tom is usually happy.

8. yes ☐   no ☐   Tom is smiling today.

9. yes ☐   no ☐   Tom's sister is studying.

      <u>VACATION</u>

10. yes ☐   no ☐   I like vacations.

11. yes ☐   no ☐   When it's hot, I read books and listen to music.

12. yes ☐   no ☐   My sister and I are playing tennis in the park.

H. LOUD AND CLEAR   Fill in the words.   Then read the sentences aloud.

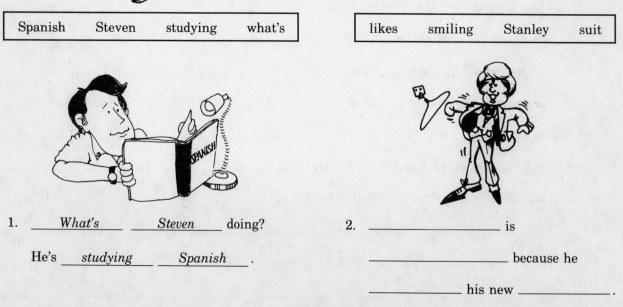

Spanish	Steven	studying	what's

likes	smiling	Stanley	suit

1. <u> *What's* </u> <u> *Steven* </u> doing?

He's <u> *studying* </u> <u> *Spanish* </u> .

2. <u>   </u> is

<u>   </u> because he

<u>   </u> his new <u>   </u>

Alice	boss	nervous	talks

3. _____ is _____

when she _____ to her

_____ .

bicycle	Stuart	school	sunny

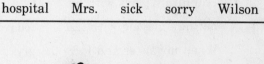

4. When it's _____ , _____

goes to _____ on his

_____ .

Sam	sister	singing	sleeping	song

5. _____ isn't _____ because

his _____ is

_____ a loud _____ .

hospital	Mrs.	sick	sorry	Wilson

6. Mr. _____ is in the

_____ . _____ Wilson is

_____ he's _____ .

Boris	bus	next	school

7. _____ always sits _____ to

the _____ driver on the _____
bus.

asks	listen	science	students	question

8. When the _____ teacher

_____ a _____ ,

her _____ always

_____ .

89

CHECK-UP TEST: *Chapters 11–12*

A. Fill in the blanks.

me	him	her	it	us	you	them

Ex. Do you like Mr. Wilson?

Of course I like *him* .

1. Does John listen to his mother?

   Of course he listens to _____ .

2. When the windows are dirty, I

   always wash _____ .

3. I don't like TV, but I'm watching

   _____ today.

4. Bob rarely plays with his brother,

   but he's playing with _____ today.

5. When my sister and I are hungry, my

   mother always feeds _____ .

B. Fill in the blanks.

Ex. I never eat breakfast, but I'm

   _____*eating*_____ breakfast today.

1. Mary never shouts, but she's

   _____ today.

2. We never _____ to the library, but
   we're going to the library today.

3. Mr. and Mrs. Jones never dance, but

   they're _____ today.

4. John never _____ his car, but
   he's fixing his car today.

5. Tommy never _____ the
   dishes, but he's washing the dishes today.

C. Fill in the blanks.

do	does	is	are

Ex. a. What _____*does*_____ Walter usually
   do on Sunday?

   b. Where _*is*_ Bobby studying?

1. When _____ Mary and Walter usually go
   to the bank?

2. Why _____ Barbara shivering?

3. _____ Bill usually wash the dishes?

4. _____ Jack and Judy cooking dinner today?

5. Do they have any pets? Yes, they _____ .

D. Write the question.

Ex. I'm crying <u>because I'm sad</u>. (Why?)

   Why are you crying?

They play tennis <u>in the park</u>. (Where?)

   Where do they play tennis?

1. She goes to the supermarket <u>on Wednesday</u>.
   (When?)

   _____

2. He's yawning <u>because he's tired</u>. (Why?)

   _____

3. They're sleeping <u>on the floor</u>. (Where?)

   _____

4. She has <u>three</u> children. (How many?)

   _____

5. I'm drinking <u>coffee</u>. (What?)

   _____

E. Listen to each question. Put a circle around the correct answer.

Ex. (a.) They're playing baseball.
   b. They play tennis.

1. a. We're dancing.
   b. We drink champagne.

2. a. I'm going to the beach.
   b. I go to school.

3. a. He's biting his nails.
   b. He eats.

4. a. She's cooking Italian food.
   b. She cooks French food.

5. a. Yes, he is.
   b. Yes, he does.

A. CAN OR CAN'T

cook	play	speak
dance	sing	swim
	skate	

1. Harry _can't_ _play_ the piano.

   He _can_ _play_ _the_ _guitar_.

2. We _____ _____.

   We _____ _____.

3. I _____ _____ chess.

   I _____ _____

   _____ .

4. Alice _____ _____.

   She _____ _____.

5. John and Robert _____

   _____ the violin.

   They _____ _____ _____

   _____ .

6. Walter _____ _____
   Italian food.

   He _____ _____ _____ _____

   _____ .

7. Mary _____ _____.

   She _____ _____.

8. Hans _____ _____ German.

   He _____ _____ _____.

91

B. WRITE ABOUT YOURSELF

What can you do?

1. I can ....

2. ....

3. ....

4. ....

5. ....

What can't you do?

1. I can't ....

2. ....

3. ....

4. ....

5. ....

C. PUZZLE

What do they do for a living?

Across

1. He drives a truck.
6. He bakes pies.
9. She acts on TV.

Down

1. He teaches in a school.
2. She fixes cars every day.
3. He dances every day.
4. She plays the violin.
5. She cooks in a restaurant.
7. He acts in the movies.
8. He sings every day.

 D. LISTEN

Listen to each sentence. Put a circle around the word you hear.

1. (can)   can't
2. can   can't
3. can   can't
4. can   can't

5. can   can't
6. can   can't
7. can   can't
8. can   can't

9. can   can't
10. can   can't
11. can   can't
12. can   can't

E. WHAT'S THE QUESTION?

1. _____*Can she bake*_____ ?
Yes, she can.

2. _____ ?
No, he can't.

3. _____ ?
Yes, they can.

4. _____ ?
Yes, I can.

5. _____ ?
No, they can't.

6. _____ ?
Yes, he can.

F. THE NELSON FAMILY

Fill in the blanks.

Sally Nelson ___*is*___ an actress. She's young and pretty, but when she acts, she can look young

or old, beautiful or _____ , happy or _____ .

Her husband, Bob, _____ an English _____. He teaches students from cities

around the world. His students speak Spanish, French, Russian, and Arabic. Bob sometimes

_____ Spanish and French with them, but he can't _____ Russian or Arabic.

Sally is a good athlete. She _____ tennis and golf very well. When it's cold she skis,

and when it's _____ she swims _____ day.

Bob doesn't like sports. He can't_____ tennis or golf, but he _____ ski. When he

isn't busy, he usually _____ the newspaper or _____ chess. He likes chess because

he _____ play very well.

Sally and Bob both love music. Sally sings popular _____ and _____ the

piano. Bob can't play the piano, but he _____ sing and he can _____ the violin.

Listen. Then clap and practice.

She can		She'kn
He can	speak =	He'kn
They can		They'kn	speak
We can		We'kn

A. Can Anne speak French?

B. Of course she can.

She can speak French very well.

A. Can the Browns play tennis?

B. Of course they can.

They can play tennis very well.

A. Can Peter bake pies?

B. Of course he can.

He can bake pies very well.

A. Can we speak English?

All. Of course we can.

We can speak English very well.

H. WHAT ARE THEY SAYING?

have to	do	don't
has to	does	doesn't

1. Why are you upset?

I _have_ _to_ go to the dentist.

2. Why is Johnny angry?

He _____ _____ clean his room.

3. Do we _____ go to the supermarket?

_____ you _____ work today?

4. No, I _____. I'm on vacation.

5. _____ I _____ wear a sweater?

Of course you _____. It's very cold today.

6. Why is Frank smiling?

He _____ _____ work on Friday.

I. A BUSY WEEK

Monday	Tuesday	Wednesday	Thursday
Tom: go to the supermarket Helen: wash the clothes	Tom and Helen : go to the dentist	Tom: clean the yard Helen: fix the car	Tom and Helen : paint the bedroom

Tom and Helen are very busy people.

1. What does Tom have to do on Monday? _____ *He has to go to the supermarket.*

2. What does Helen have to do on Wednesday? _____

3. What does Helen have to do on Monday? _____

4. What do Tom and Helen have to do on Thursday? _____

5. What do Tom and Helen have to do on Tuesday? _____

6. What does Tom have to do on Wednesday? _____

J. WRITE ABOUT YOURSELF

What do YOU have to do this week?

....

....

....

....

....

....

....

....

....

can't	do the laundry	go skiing	play cards
have to	fix the TV	go swimming	play tennis
has to	go dancing	go to the dentist	study
	go jogging	go to the doctor	teach
	go sailing	go to the zoo	wash the kitchen floor
			work

1. John _____ *can't go skiing* today.
    He _____ *has to study* _____ .

2. Richard and Alice _____ today.
    They _____ .

3. Mrs. Smith _____ today.
    She _____ .

4. I _____ today.
    I _____ .

5. Paul _____ today.
    He _____ .

6. Mrs. Wilson _____ today.
    She _____ .

7. We _____ today.
    We _____ .

8. Mrs. Brown _____ today.
    She _____ .

97

L. RHYTHM AND RHYME: *Where Is Everybody?*

Listen. Then clap and practice.

A. Where's   Joe?

B. He has to   go.

A. Where's   Ray?

B. He can't   stay.

A. Where's   Kate?

B. She can't   wait.

A. Where's   Steve?

B. He has to   leave.

A. Where's   Murray?

B. He has to   hurry.

A. What about   you?

B. I have to go, too.

All. Oh,   no!

Joe has to   go.

Ray can't   stay.

Kate can't   wait.

Steve has to   leave.

Murray has to hurry.

What can I   do?

I have to go, too.

M. RHYTHM AND RHYME: *Can't Talk Now*

Listen. Then clap and practice.

A. I can't talk   now.

I have to go to   work.

B. I can't stop   now.

I have to catch a train.

C. I can't leave   now.

I have to make a call.

D. I can't stop   now.

I have to catch a plane.

All. He can't stop   now.

He has to catch a train.

He can't stop   now.

He has to catch a plane.

A. WHAT ARE THEY GOING TO DO?

1. What's Sally going to do this afternoon?

   She's going to study English.

2. What are Mr. and Mrs. Green going to do tomorrow morning?

   _____

3. What's Helen going to do tomorrow afternoon?

   _____

4. What are you and George going to do this morning?

   _____

5. What's your grandfather going to do this evening?

   _____

6. What are Stuart and Doris going to do today?

   _____

7. _____ Linda _____ tonight?

   _____

8. _____ you _____ this evening?

   _____

99

Listen. Then clap and practice.

> going to = gónna

All.
• • • •
What are you going to do tomorrow morning?

• • •
How about tomorrow afternoon?

• • • •
What are you going to do tomorrow evening?

• • • •
What are you going to do this June?

•
A. I'm going to vacuum all my rugs tomorrow morning.

•
B. I'm going to walk my dog tomorrow afternoon.

•
C. I'm going to visit all my friends tomorrow evening.

•
D. I'm going to dance at my wedding this June.

■□ **C. RHYTHM AND RHYME:** *I Don't Have a Clue!*

Listen. Then clap and practice.

A. What's he going to do?   A. When's she going to leave?

B. Where's he going to go?   B. Where's she going to be?

C. Who's he going to see?   C. How's she going to go?

All. I don't know.   All. Don't ask me.

A. Why are they going to come here?

B. What are they going to do?

C. When are they going to get here?

All. I don't have a clue!

D. AN INTERNATIONAL MOVIE ACTOR

JANUARY - Rome
FEBRUARY - Geneva
APRIL - London
JUNE - Honolulu
SEPTEMBER - TOKYO

George Dupont is a famous international movie actor. He lives in Paris, but he always works in cities around the world.

Next January, George is going to act in Rome. He's glad he's going to work there because he loves Italian music. In the evening when he isn't busy, he's going to go to concerts.

Next February, George is going skiing in Geneva with his wife and son. George always goes skiing on his winter vacation, and he always has a wonderful time.

Next April, George is going to work in London. His wife and son are going to visit him every weekend. When they're together, they're going to go shopping in expensive London stores, and his son is going to go to the London Zoo.

Next June, George and his family are going to Honolulu on their summer vacation. They love the beautiful beaches there, and they're going to go swimming and sailing every day.

Next September, George is going to Tokyo. He's going to act in a Japanese movie. His family can't go with him, but he isn't upset because his son and wife are going to write to him from Paris. When he isn't working, he's going to go to Japanese restaurants and baseball games with his friends.

1. When is George going to Rome? _____ *He's going to Rome next January.* _____

2. What's he going to do in Rome in the evening? _____

_____

3. When are George and his family going to Geneva? _____

_____

4. What are they going to do there? _____

_____

5. Where is George going to work next April? _____

6. What are George and his family going to do in London? _____

_____

7. When are George and his family going to Honolulu? _____

_____

8. What are they going to do there? _____

9. When is George going to Tokyo? _____

10. Why is George going to Tokyo? _____

11. What's he going to do there when he isn't working? _____

_____

E. WHAT'S THE QUESTION?

1. I'm going to <u>fix my car</u> this afternoon.   (What?)   *What are you going to do this afternoon?*

2. He's going to cut his hair <u>next week</u>.   (When?) _____

3. They're going to <u>Madrid</u> next summer.   (Where?) _____

   _____

4. She's going to plant flowers <u>this spring</u>.   (When?) _____

5. He's going to visit his grandmother <u>because she's sick</u>.   (Why?) _____

   _____

6. They're going to <u>write to their brother</u> this morning.   (What?) _____

   _____

7. I'm going to call the plumber <u>right away</u>.   (When?) _____

8. He's going to eat <u>at a restaurant</u> tonight.   (Where?) _____

   _____

▭ F. LISTEN

Listen to the following weather forecasts.   Put a circle around the correct answer.   You will hear each forecast twice.

TODAY'S WEATHER FORECAST

1. This afternoon:

   (warm)   cool   (sunny)   cloudy   rain

2. This evening:

   warm   cool   sunny   cloudy   rain

THIS WEEKEND'S FORECAST

3. Tonight:

   cool   cold   sunny   clear   foggy

4. Saturday:

   cool   cold   sunny   clear   foggy

5. Sunday:

   cool   cold   sunny   clear   foggy

MONDAY'S WEATHER FORECAST

6. Monday morning:

   cool   cold   sunny   cloudy   snow

7. Monday afternoon and evening:

   cool   cold   sunny   cloudy   snow

8. Tuesday:

   cool   cold   sunny   cloudy   snow

102

G. BAD WEATHER

go skating	paint the house	be cloudy
go to a baseball game	wash the car	be cold
go to the park		be warm
have a picnic		rain
		snow

1. What do Shirley and Patty want to
   do tomorrow?

   They want to go skating.

   What's the forecast?

   It's going to be warm.

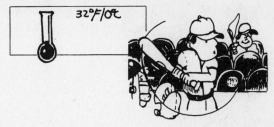

2. What does Jeff want to do tomorrow?

   _____

   What's the forecast?

   _____

3. What do Gloria and Frank want to do
   tomorrow?

   _____

   What's the forecast?

   _____

4. What does Lois want to do tomorrow?

   _____

   What's the forecast?

   _____

5. What do Anita and Ted want to do
   tomorrow?

   _____

   What's the forecast?

   _____

6. What does Sam want to do tomorrow?

   _____

   What's the forecast?

   _____

103

H. YES AND NO

doesn't want to
don't want to

YES!		NO!
1. John wants to play chess.		_He doesn't want to play_ _____ checkers.
2. Mary wants to go to the zoo.		_____ to a concert.
3. I want to visit my friend.		_____ my grandmother.
4. Mr. and Mrs. Smith want to eat dinner at a restaurant.		_____ dinner at home.
5. We want to study Arabic.		_____ mathematics.
6. Our English cousins want to drink tea.		_____ coffee.
7. Bob wants to dance with Lois.		_____ with his sister.

I. YES AND NO

I'm	not	
He		
She	isn't	
It		going to
We		
You	aren't	
They		

YES!		NO!
1. Bill is going to call his uncle.		_He isn't going to call_ _____ his mother.
2. I'm going to fix the TV.		_____ the sink.
3. We're going to go skating.		_____ skiing.
4. My aunt and uncle are going to live in London.		_____ in Berlin.
5. Mr. Jones is going to listen to music.		_____ to the forecast.
6. It's going to be cloudy.		_____ sunny.
7. Alice is going to cook dinner.		_____ lunch.

104

J. FUTURE HOPES

Sally is a mechanic, but she wants to be a teacher.   She wants to teach English in Mexico City.

1.   ___*What*___ ___*does*___ Sally ___*want*___ ___*to*___ be?

   ___*She*___ ___*wants*___ ___*to*___ ___*be*___ a teacher.

2.   _____ _____ she _____ _____ teach?

   _____ _____ _____ _____ English.

3.   _____ _____ she _____ _____ work?

   _____ _____ _____ _____ in Mexico City.

Arthur is a teacher, but he wants to be a mechanic.   He wants to work in a garage and fix cars.

4.   _____ _____ Arthur _____ _____ be?

   _____ _____ _____ _____ a mechanic.

5.   _____ _____ he _____ _____ do?

   _____ _____ _____ fix cars.

6.   _____ _____ he _____ _____ work?

   _____ _____ _____ _____ in a garage.

K.   WRITE ABOUT YOURSELF

What do you want to be?   What do you want to do?   Where do you want to work?

....

....

....

....

....

L. PRONUNCIATION: *What Do They Want to Do?*

Listen. Then clap and practice.

want to = wánna	wants to = wántsta

He wants to   go.

I want to   stay.

He wants to   work.

I want to   play.

She wants to   eat at a   restaurant.

I want to   eat at   home.

She wants to   eat with   all our   friends.

I want to   eat   alone.

We want to   leave at   seven.

They want to   leave at   eight.

We want to   get there   early.

They want to   get there   late.

Jack wants to take the   eight o'clock plane.

Joe wants to   take the   bus.

Bob wants to take the   six o'clock   train.

Bill wants to come with   us.

106

M. WHAT TIME IS IT?

Draw the time on the clocks.

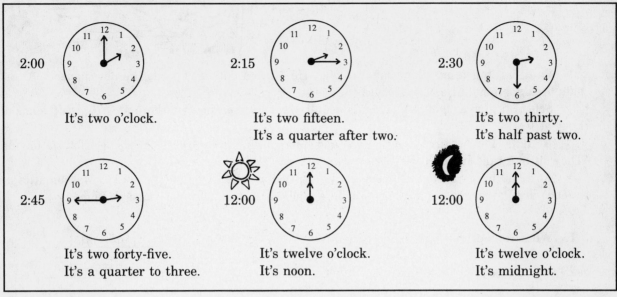

2:00 — It's two o'clock.

2:15 — It's two fifteen. It's a quarter after two.

2:30 — It's two thirty. It's half past two.

2:45 — It's two forty-five. It's a quarter to three.

12:00 — It's twelve o'clock. It's noon.

12:00 — It's twelve o'clock. It's midnight.

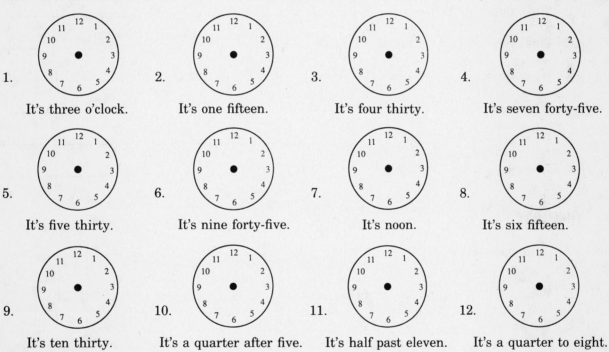

1. It's three o'clock.

2. It's one fifteen.

3. It's four thirty.

4. It's seven forty-five.

5. It's five thirty.

6. It's nine forty-five.

7. It's noon.

8. It's six fifteen.

9. It's ten thirty.

10. It's a quarter after five.

11. It's half past eleven.

12. It's a quarter to eight.

N. LISTEN

Listen and write the time you hear.

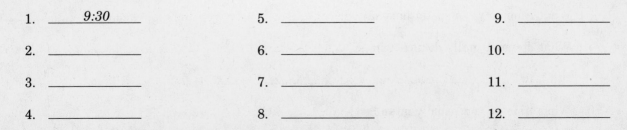

1. _9:30_

2. _____

3. _____

4. _____

5. _____

6. _____

7. _____

8. _____

9. _____

10. _____

11. _____

12. _____

O. PAUL SMITH'S DAY

Paul Smith gets up every day at 8:00. He takes a bath and reads the newspaper. At 8:30 he eats breakfast, and at 8:45 he leaves the house.

School begins at 9:00, and Paul is usually late. When he gets there at 9:15, his friends are busy at work.

At 12:00 Paul is tired and hungry, and he and his friends go to the school cafeteria for lunch. They sit and talk and do their homework.

At 12:30 Paul's mathematics class begins, and at 2:00 he studies science. Mathematics and science are Paul's favorite subjects, but he's glad when it's 3:00 and he can go home.

1. What time does Paul get up every day? _____ *He gets up at 8:00.* _____

2. What does he do at 8:30? _____

3. What time does he leave the house? _____

4. What time does school begin? _____

5. What time does he eat lunch? _____

6. What time does his mathematics class begin? _____

7. What does he do at 2:00? _____

8. What does he do at 3:00? _____

P. YOUR DAY

Answer in complete sentences.

1. What time do you usually get up? _____

2. What do you do after you get up? _____

3. What time do you usually leave for school/work? _____

4. What time do you usually have lunch? _____

5. What time do you get home from school/work? _____

6. What time do you usually have dinner? _____

7. What do you usually do after dinner? _____

    _____

8. What time do you usually go to bed? _____

Listen.   Then clap and practice.

Time   flies.

The days go by.

Monday   morning,

Tuesday,   Wednesday,

Thursday,   Friday,   Saturday,   Sunday.

Time   flies.

The days go by.

Time   flies.

The months go by.

January,   February,   March,   April.

Time   flies,   the months go by.

May,   June,   July,   August.

Time   flies.

The months go by.

September, October,   November,   December.

The seasons come,

The seasons go.

Autumn,   winter,

Spring,   summer.

Time   flies.

The years go by.

Where do they go?

I don't   know.

A.

Ex. John _____*wants to go skiing*_____, but

_____*he can't*_____. He _____*has to study*_____.

1. Bob and Jane _____, but

_____. They _____.

2. I _____, but

_____. I _____.

3. Mrs. Brown _____, but

_____. She _____.

B. Fill in the blanks.

is	are	do	does

Ex. When ___*is*___ Bob going to eat dinner?

1. When _____ you going to wash your clothes?

2. _____ I have to go to the doctor?

3. What _____ Mary have to do this week?

4. Where _____ you want to live?

5. What _____ Mr. and Mrs. Jones going to do tomorrow?

6. When _____ Robert going to go to London?

C. *Ex.* Janet wants to drink champagne.   _____*She doesn't want to drink*_____ lemonade.

Peter is going to fix the sink.   _____*He isn't going to fix*_____ the car.

1. Bob wants to study English.   _____ French.

2. We're going to get up at 8:00.   _____ at 9:00.

3. Sally and Fred can play soccer.   _____ tennis.

4. I'm going to wash the dishes.   _____ the clothes.

5. Ted can speak Russian.   _____ Swedish.

6. Judy has to cook dinner.   _____ lunch.

110

D.   Every day Charlie eats breakfast at 7:00.   At 7:30 he washes the dishes, and at 8:00 he goes to work.   At 12:00 Charlie reads the newspaper, and at 12:30 he calls his wife.

   What's Charlie going to do tomorrow?

   Tomorrow Charlie _____*is going to eat*_____ breakfast at 7:00.   At 7:30 he's

_____ the dishes, and at 8:00 _____ to

work.   At 12:00 _____ the newspaper, and at 12:30

_____ his wife.

E.   Write the question.

What	When	Where

Ex. I'm going to fix my car <u>next week</u>.   _____*When are you going to fix your car?*_____

1.   He's going to <u>plant flowers</u> tomorrow.   _____

2.   They're going to work <u>in Boston</u>
     next summer.   _____

3.   She's going to study <u>Spanish</u>
     next year.   _____

4.   I'm going to visit my uncle
     <u>next week</u>.   _____

F.   What time is it?

Ex.   It's three o'clock.

1.   It's two thirty.

2.   It's four fifteen.

3.   It's six forty-five.

4.   It's noon.

5.   It's a quarter after seven.

G.   Listen to the story.   Fill in the correct times.

English	_8:15_	French	_____
mathematics	_____	science	_____
lunch	_____	music	_____

A. ALL MY FRIENDS ARE SICK TODAY

backache	earache	sore throat	toothache
cold	headache	stomachache	

 John
 Margaret
 Walter
 Hilda
 Linda
 George

1. What's the matter with John? _He has a toothache._

2. What's the matter with Linda? _____

3. _____ Walter? _____

4. _____ Margaret? _____

5. _____ George? _____

6. _____ Hilda? _____

7. What's the matter with you? _____

 B. LISTEN

Listen to the story. Write the correct number next to each picture.

1

Listen. Then clap and practice.

A. What's the matter with you?

B. I have a headache.

What's the matter with YOU?

A. I have a cold.

A. What's the matter with Fred?

B. He has a backache.

What's the matter with ANNE?

A. She has an awful cold.

A. What's the matter with him?

B. He has a toothache.

What's the matter with HER?

A. She has a cold.

A. What's the matter with Jane?

B. She has a stomachache.

What's the matter with PAUL?

A. He has a terrible cold.

A. What's the matter with Mary?

B. She has an earache.

What's the matter with BILL?

A. He has a very bad cold.

A. What's the matter with the students?

B. They have sore throats.

What's the matter with the teachers?

A. They have terrible colds.

They have terrible, terrible colds!

113

D. WHAT DID YOU DO YESTERDAY?

Write the sentence and then say it.

clean	listen	skate	wash
cook	paint	study	watch
fix	plant	visit	work
	play		

1. _____*I played*_____ the piano.

2. _____ at the office.

3. _____ my living room.

4. _____ TV.

5. _____ English.

6. _____ my apartment.

7. _____ flowers.

8. _____ dinner.

114

9. _____

10. _____ my car.

11. _____ my friend in
the hospital.

12. _____ to the radio
and _____ my
clothes.

🖭 **E. LISTEN**

Listen to each sentence.   Put a circle around the correct word.

Ex. I play baseball.   ┌─────────────┐   I played baseball.   ┌─────────────┐
                         │ yesterday   │   │ (yesterday) │
                         │ (every day) │   │ every day │
                         └─────────────┘   └─────────────┘

1.	yesterday / every day	6.	yesterday / every day	11.	yesterday / every day
2.	yesterday / every day	7.	yesterday / every day	12.	yesterday / every day
3.	yesterday / every day	8.	yesterday / every day	13.	yesterday / every day
4.	yesterday / every day	9.	yesterday / every day	14.	yesterday / every day
5.	yesterday / every day	10.	yesterday / every day	15.	yesterday / every day

F. JOHN'S DAY AT HOME

bake	cook	fix	paint	plant	rest	wash

John worked at home all day.   His family is very happy.

1.  Thank you, John. This is a very good dinner.

2. This is a wonderful apple pie, John.

3. The new flowers in the garden are beautiful.

4. Look at the car. It's really clean. Thank you.

5. The bedroom looks beautiful.   Blue is my favorite color.

6. The TV isn't broken! I can watch my favorite TV program tonight.

What did John do?

1. _____ *He cooked dinner.* _____

2. _____

3. _____

4. _____

5. _____

6. _____

What did John do after dinner?

7. _____

G. WHAT DID EVERYBODY DO?

bake	play baseball	wait for the bus
dance	skate	work
paint the bathroom	study	

1. What did David do today?

   _____ *He worked* _____ all day.

2. What did Billy and his father do yesterday?

   _____

   all afternoon.

3. What did Fred do yesterday?

_____

all afternoon.

4. What did Mr. and Mrs. Smith do yesterday?

_____

all evening.

5. What did Shirley do today?

_____

all afternoon.

6. What did you and your husband do yesterday?

_____

all afternoon.

7. _____ Nancy _____ today?

_____ all afternoon.

8. _____ Mr. and Mrs. Wilson

_____ yesterday?

_____ all day.

Listen. Then clap and practice.

| washed [t] | cleaned [d] | painted [ɪd] |

A. What did you do today?

B. I washed my floors.

A. Your floors? B. Yes!

I washed my floors all day!

A. What did Mark do today?

B. He cleaned his house.

A. His house? B. Yes!

He cleaned his house all day!

A. What did Pam do today?

B. She painted her porch.

A. Her porch? B. Yes!

She painted her porch all day!

A. What did they do today?

B. They sang some songs.

A. Some songs? B. Yes!

They sang some songs all day!

A. What did you do today?

B. I _____.

A. _____? B. Yes!

I _____ all day!

I. BILL'S WEDDING

Fill in the missing words.

At Bill's wedding last night, my father (play) _____played_____ the piano, and my mother
                                                        1

(sing) _____ popular songs.   My little sister Sara (eat) _____ cookies and candy all
              2   3

night.

My brother Peter is a wonderful dancer.   Last night he (dance) _____ with all my
                                                                          4

cousins and all my aunts.

Aunt Helen and Uncle David always sit and talk at parties.   At Bill's wedding they

(sit) _____ on the sofa together and (talk) _____ about their children all night.
            5   6

Bill's grandmother (sit) _____ next to them and (cry) _____.
                              7   8

What did I do at Bill's wedding?   I (eat) _____ a lot of food, I (drink) _____
                                                  9   10

champagne, and I (talk) _____ with EVERYBODY at the wedding.
                              11

J. THE DAY AFTER BILL'S WEDDING

1. Peter has a backache this morning.   Why?

    _____*Because he danced with all his cousins and all his aunts last night.*_____

2. Sara has a stomachache this morning.   Why?

    _____

3. Aunt Helen has a sore throat this morning.   Why?

    _____

4. I have a sore throat this morning.   Why?

    _____

A. CORRECT THE SENTENCE

1. My sister fixed the TV this morning.

    She didn't fix the TV.

    She fixed the car.

3. William washed the clothes this morning.

_____

5. Bob talked to his uncle yesterday evening.

_____

_____

7. Maria studied mathematics this evening.

_____

_____

2. Mr. and Mrs. Nelson painted their bedroom yesterday morning.

_____

_____

4. Our neighbors played chess yesterday evening.

_____

6. Peggy waited for the train this morning.

_____

_____

8. Mr. Jones called the doctor yesterday afternoon.

_____

_____

120

Listen to the story.   Write the missing words.

Sally is very tired today.   She ___worked___ all day yesterday, and her family didn't
_____ her.   Yesterday morning she _____ the car.   Yesterday afternoon she
_____ the bathroom.   Yesterday evening she _____ the basement.   She didn't
_____ all day.

Sally's brother isn't very tired today.   Yesterday he didn't _____.   He didn't
_____ the car.   He didn't _____ the bathroom, and he didn't _____
the basement.   What did he do?   He _____ on the telephone all morning.   He
_____ to music all afternoon, and he _____ in front of the TV all evening.

C.   WRITE ABOUT SALLY AND HER BROTHER

1.   Did Sally work all day yesterday?   ___*Yes, she did.*___

2.   Did her brother work all day yesterday?   _____

3.   Did Sally fix the car yesterday morning?   _____

4.   Did her brother talk on the telephone yesterday morning?   _____

5.   Did Sally talk on the telephone yesterday morning?   _____

6.   ___*Did Sally fix*___ the car yesterday morning?   Yes, she did.

7.   _____ the bathroom yesterday afternoon?   Yes, she did.

8.   _____ to music yesterday afternoon?   Yes, he did.

9.   _____ the basement after dinner?   No, he didn't.

10.   _____ in front of the TV yesterday evening?   No, she didn't.

11.   _____ the basement yesterday evening?   Yes, she did.

121

D. YESTERDAY

1. Henry usually takes the bus.

He _didn't_ _take_ the bus yesterday.

He _took_ the subway.

2. Julie usually buys candy.

She _____ _____ candy yesterday.

She _____ cookies.

3. Mr. and Mrs. Smith usually go jogging.

They _____ _____ jogging yesterday.

They _____ swimming.

4. Sara usually writes to her mother.

She _____ _____ to her mother yesterday.

She _____ to her father.

5. Peter and George usually get up at 7:00.

They _____ _____ _____ at 7:00 yesterday.

They _____ _____ at 9:00.

6. I usually have dinner at 6:00.

I _____ _____ dinner at 6:00 yesterday.

I _____ dinner at 8:00.

7. Paul usually reads novels.

He _____ _____ a novel yesterday.

He _____ poetry.

8. George and Peter usually do their homework at 4:00.

They _____ _____ their homework at 4:00 yesterday.

They _____ their homework after dinner.

9. Charlie usually eats at home.

He _____ _____ at home yesterday.

He _____ at a Chinese restaurant.

10. I usually drink tea.

I _____ _____ tea yesterday.

I _____ coffee.

11. Walter usually sits next to John.

He _____ _____ next to John yesterday.

He _____ next to Nancy.

12. David and Barbara usually sing popular songs.

They _____ _____ popular songs yesterday.

They _____ old songs.

13. Jane usually takes a shower.

She _____ _____ a shower yesterday.

She _____ a bath.

14. We usually go to a movie on Saturday.

We _____ _____ to a movie yesterday.

We _____ to a concert.

15. Mr. and Mrs. Wilson usually buy Mexican coffee.

They _____ _____ Mexican coffee yesterday.

They _____ French coffee.

16. Jim usually has lunch with his brother.

He _____ _____ lunch with his brother yesterday.

He _____ lunch with his boss.

E. RHYMING GAME: *No, They Didn't*

Fill in the missing words with words that rhyme. Then clap and practice.

A. Did she wash her skirt?

B. No, she didn't.

A. What did she wash?

B. She washed her *shirt* .

A. Did they paint the floor?

B. No, they didn't.

A. What did they paint?

B. They painted the _____ .

A. Did he call his mother?

B. No, he didn't.

A. Who did he call?

B. He called his _____ .

A. Did you buy potatoes?

B. No, we didn't.

A. What did you buy?

B. We bought _____ .

A. Did you get up at seven?

B. No, I didn't.

A. When did you get up?

B. I got up at _____ .

F. WHAT'S THE QUESTION?

1. _Did you go_ to the bank?   No, I didn't.   I went to the post office.

2. _____ a car?   No, he didn't.   He bought a bicycle.

3. _____ to their uncle?   No, they didn't.   They wrote to their sister.

4. _____ a stomachache?   No, she didn't.   She had a cold.

5. _____ at 9:00?   No, I didn't.   I got up at 11:00.

6. _____ today's newspaper?   No, I didn't.   I read yesterday's newspaper.

7. _____ bowling?   No, we didn't.   We went dancing.

8. _____ a good time?   No, they didn't.   They had a terrible time.

9. _____ Italian food?   No, we didn't.   We ate Greek food.

10. _____ a new shirt?   No, he didn't.   He bought a new tie.

11. _____ coffee?   No, they didn't.   They drank tea.

12. _____ French songs?   No, she didn't.   She sang German songs.

13. _____ her Spanish homework?   No, she didn't.   She did her English homework.

14. _____ next to Robert?   No, I didn't.   I sat next to Fred.

G. LISTEN

Listen to each question.   Put a circle around the correct answer.

1. a. She goes to the bank on Friday.
   b. She went to the bank yesterday.

2. a. He studies French.
   b. He studied Spanish.

3. a. He does his homework at 4:00.
   b. He did his homework after dinner.

4. a. I buy tomatoes.
   b. I bought bananas.

5. a. I listen to popular music.
   b. I listened to rock music.

6. a. He visits his uncle.
   b. He visited his aunt.

7. a. She writes to her grandmother every week.
   b. She wrote to her grandmother yesterday.

8. a. They play basketball at school.
   b. They played basketball in the park.

9. a. They go dancing on Saturday.
   b. They went dancing last night.

10. a. He cleans his room on Friday.
    b. He cleaned his room this morning.

H. BUT THEY DIDN'T

Bill went to a restaurant yesterday afternoon, but he didn't eat.   He drank coffee, and he studied mathematics.

1. Where _did_ Bill _go_ yesterday afternoon?   _He went_ to a restaurant.

2. What _____ he _drink_ ?   _____ coffee.

3. What _____ he _____ ?   _____ mathematics.

Alice went to the supermarket yesterday, but she didn't buy any food.   She forgot her purse and had to call her mother.

4. Where _____ Alice _____ yesterday?   _____ to the supermarket.

5. What _____ she _____ ?   _____ her purse.

6. Who _____ she _____ ?   _____ her mother.

Steven and Nancy went to their science class this morning, but they didn't study science. They ate candy and listened to records at a birthday party for their teacher.

7. When _____ Steven and Nancy   _____ this morning.

_____ to their science class?

8. What _____ they _____ ?   _____ candy.

9. What _____ they _____ to?   _____ to records.

Mary went to a night club last Saturday, but she didn't dance.   She met an old friend, and they talked all night.

10. When _____ Mary _____ to a night club?   _____ last Saturday.

11. Who _____ she _____ ?   _____ an old friend.

12. What _____ they do?   _____ all night.

Listen and recite.

Old Friends

We walked and talked
And talked and walked.
Walked and talked,
Talked and walked.

We sat in a garden
And looked at the flowers.
We talked and talked
For hours and hours.

He drank coffee
And I drank tea.
We talked and talked
From one to three.

We talked about him.
We talked about us.
Then we walked to the corner
To get the bus.

We waited and waited.
The bus was late.
So we stood and talked
From four to eight.

Gossip

I told Jack.
Jack told Jill.
Jill told Fred.
Fred told Bill.
Bill called Anne.
Anne called Sue.
Sue told Jim.
But who told you?

A. A TERRIBLE MORNING

was	were

I _____ very depressed last Monday.   The weather _____ terrible.   It _____ cold and
       1   2   3

foggy.   My husband _____ sick, and the neighbors _____ angry because my children _____
                         4   5   6

noisy.

The house _____ dirty.   There _____ dishes in the sink.   My children's clothes
              7   8

_____ on the floor in their bedroom, and our refrigerator _____ broken.   I _____ tired
          9   10   11

and hungry all morning.

B. A BEAUTIFUL MORNING

was	were

I _____ very happy yesterday morning.   The weather _____ beautiful.   It _____ warm and
       1   2   3

sunny.   There _____ flowers in the garden.   There _____ a bird at the window.   My
                         4   5

children _____ at school, and my husband and I _____ on vacation.
               6   7

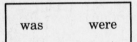 C. LISTEN

Listen to each sentence.   Put a circle around the word you hear.

1.
(is)
was

2.
is
was

3.
are
were

4.
is
was

5.
is
was

6.
are
were

7.
are
were

8.
are
were

9.
is
was

10.
is
was

11.
are
were

12.
are
were

127

D. BEFORE AND NOW

beautiful	expensive	heavy
cold	full	tired
dirty	happy	quiet

1.

Before I painted my room, it *was* ugly.

Now *it's* *beautiful* .

2.

Before I worked at Stanley's Restaurant,

I _____ thin.

Now _____ _____ .

3.

Last week the weather _____ warm.

Now _____ _____ .

4.

Before Mary met her husband, she _____ always sad.

Now _____ _____ .

5.

When our children _____ young,

they _____ always noisy.

Now _____ _____ .

6.

Before we had dinner, we _____ hungry.

Now _____ _____ .

7.

When I _____ young, coffee _____ cheap.

Now _____ _____ .

8.

Before Jack worked in a garage, his clothes _____ always clean.

Now _____ _____ .

9.

Before we got married, you _____ energetic.

Now _____ always _____ .

128

E. A THIEF STOLE A CAR

was	were	wasn't	weren't

A thief stole an expensive car from a garage on Main Street last Sunday at 5:00. Mr. and Mrs. Jones _were_ in a restaurant next to the garage. Charlie Green _____ across the street in
1   2
a grocery store.

According to Mr. and Mrs. Jones, the thief _____ tall and thin. His hair _____ brown
3   4
and curly. According to Charlie Green, the thief _____ young and handsome. His clothes
5
_____ expensive.
6

The police are looking for the thief today. They're talking to Frank Harris. He's a tall, thin young man with brown, curly hair.

Police: _____ you on Main Street last Sunday at 5:00?
        7

Frank: No, I _____. I _____ at home with my wife.
              8   9

Police: Are you sure?

Frank: Of course I am.

Police: That's strange. Your wife says she _____ at home all evening, but you
                                       10
_____ there.
11

Frank: I wasn't?!

Police: No, you _____.
            12

Frank: Oh, I forgot. Last Sunday at 5:00 I _____ with my friend Tom.
                                        13

Police: Where _____ you and your friend?
               14

Frank: We _____ here at the police station.
           15

Police: Why _____ you at the police station?
           16

Frank: We _____ here because at 4:00 last Sunday a thief stole my friend Tom's
           17
car!

1. According to Mr. and Mrs. Jones, was the thief tall and thin? _____ _Yes, he was._

2. Was his hair blond and straight? _____

3. According to Charlie Green, was the thief old? _____

4. Were his clothes expensive? _____

5. Was Frank at home at 5:00 last Sunday? _____

6. Was he with his wife? _____

7. Who was he with? _____

8. Where were they? _____

9. Why? _____

F. ROBERT'S PARTY

Robert had a big party last night.
His friends are talking about the party today.

1.

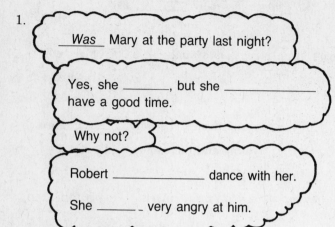

___Was___ Mary at the party last night?

Yes, she _____, but she _____ have a good time.

Why not?

Robert _____ dance with her.

She _____ very angry at him.

2.

_____ you have a good time at the party last night?

No, I _____.

Why not?

I _____ like the music.

It _____ very loud.

3.

_____ Fred and Tom at the party?

No, they _____.

Why not?

Fred _____ feel well, and

Tom _____ busy.

4.

Why _____ you upset last night?

I missed the train, and I _____ late. When

I arrived at the party, there _____

any food. I _____ hungry all night.

6.

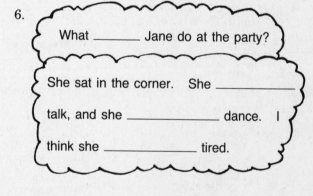

What _____ Jane do at the party?

She sat in the corner. She _____

talk, and she _____ dance. I

think she _____ tired.

5.

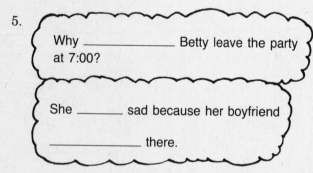

Why _____ Betty leave the party at 7:00?

She _____ sad because her boyfriend

_____ there.

7.

_____ you like Robert's party?

Yes, I _____. The food and the

music _____ wonderful, and

all my friends _____ there.

G. RHYTHM AND RHYME: *Were You Late This Morning?*

Listen. Then clap and practice.

A.	Were you late this	morning?
B.	No, I wasn't. I was	early.
A.	Was he sick last	night?
B.	No, he wasn't. He was	fine.
A.	Was her hair very	straight?
B.	No, it wasn't. It was	curly.
A.	Were there eight new	lessons?
B.	No, there weren't. There were	nine.
A.	Was the movie	short?
B.	No, it wasn't. It was	long.
A.	Was the wine	expensive?
B.	No, it wasn't. It was	free.
A.	Was I right?	
B.	No, you weren't. You were	wrong.
A.	Were the tickets two	dollars?
B.	No, they weren't. They were three.	

131

H. LISTEN: *Julie and Her Grandparents*

Listen to the conversation.   Fill in the missing words.

A. How __old__ _____were_____ you when you _____met_____ Grandmother?

B. I _____ _____ years old, and she _____ eleven.

A. Where _____ you _____?

B. We _____ to school together, and I _____ _____ to your grandmother in science class.

A. _____ you _____ her with her science homework?

B. No, I _____. She _____ me.   She _____ a very good student, but I

_____ .

1. How old was Julie's grandfather when he met Julie's grandmother?

   _____

2. Where did they meet?

   _____

3. Where did Julie's grandfather sit in science class?

   _____

4. Did Julie's grandfather help his grandmother with her science homework?

   _____

5. Why not?

   _____

I. LISTEN: *Miss Gaylord*

Listen to the conversation.   Fill in the missing words.

A. Miss Gaylord.   What _____ you _____ like when you _____ a child?   _____ you

very beautiful?   _____ you _____ many boyfriends?

B. My _____ were pretty, but I _____ short and heavy.   I _____ straight brown

_____ and freckles.   I _____ like boys, and they _____ _____

me.   When I _____ to _____ , I _____ always embarrassed.

1. Was Miss Gaylord beautiful when she was young? _____

2. Were her sisters pretty? _____

3. What did Miss Gaylord look like? _____

   _____

4. Did she like boys? _____

5. When was she always embarrassed? _____

   _____

J. LISTEN: *Grandchildren*

Listen to the conversation. Fill in the missing words.

A. How _____ _____ Tommy when he began to _____?

B. He _____ _____ months old, and I _____ him his first pair _____ shoes. When

   he began to _____, his first words _____ "_____" and "_____."

A. Really? _____ I tell you about my grandson Jimmy? He was _____ _____

   old when he _____ _____ _____.

B. Yes, you _____, but that's okay. I love to hear about Jimmy. _____ old _____ he now?

A. He's _____ _____ old.

1. How old was Tommy when he began to walk?

   _____

2. What were his first words? _____

3. How old was Jimmy when he began to walk? _____

4. How old is Jimmy now? _____

133

K. RHYTHM AND RHYME: *The Teacher Was There*

Listen.   Then clap and practice.

A.   The teacher was   there,

But where were the   students?

B.   The students were   there.

All.   Where?

A.   The teacher was   there,

The students were   there,

But where were the   books?

B.   The books were   there.

All.   Where?

A.   The teacher was   there,

The students were   there,

The books were   there,

But where was the   chalk?

B.   The chalk was   there.

All.   Where?

A.   The teacher was   there,

The students were   there,

The books were   there,

The chalk was   there,

But where were the chairs?

B.   The chairs were   there.

All.   Where?

B.   There.

All.   Where?

B.   Right there!

Right   there!

A. Fill in the blanks.

| was | were | wasn't | weren't |

1. A. _Was_ John at school yesterday?

   B. No, he _____. He _____ sick.

2. A. Why _____ Jane and Betty upset?

   B. They _____ upset because the weather _____ good.

3. A. Where _____ you and Lois last night? I called you, but you _____ at home.

   B. We _____ at the movies.

B. Complete the sentences.

Ex. Before we painted the living room, it _was_ ugly. Now _it's_ _beautiful_ .

1. Before I worked at Stanley's Restaurant, I _____ thin. Now _____ _____.

2. When Mr. and Mrs. Smith got married, they _____ poor. Now _____ _____.

3. When we _____ young, we _____ energetic. Now _____ always

   _____ .

C. Complete the sentences.

Ex. a. Barbara usually bakes cookies.

   She _didn't_ _bake_ cookies yesterday.

   She _baked_ an apple pie.

   b. Robert usually writes to his father.

   He _didn't_ _write_ to his father yesterday.

   He _wrote_ to his grandfather.

1. I usually have lunch at school.

   I _____ _____ lunch at school yesterday.

   I _____ lunch at home.

2. We usually listen to records.

   We _____ _____ to records yesterday.

   We _____ to the radio.

3. George and Paul usually visit their uncle.

   They _____ _____ their uncle yesterday.

   They _____ their aunt.

4. Jack usually goes jogging.

   He _____ _____ jogging yesterday.

   He _____ swimming.

D. Write the question.

Ex. _____*Did you get up*_____ at 9:00?   No, I didn't.   I got up at 10:00.

1. _____ to her uncle?   No, she didn't.   She wrote to her brother.

2. _____ baseball?   No, I didn't.   I played tennis.

3. _____ a good time?   No, they didn't.   They had a terrible time.

4. _____ the newspaper?   No, she didn't.   She read a book.

5. _____ to the movies?   No, he didn't.   He went to a concert.

E. Read the story and then write about yesterday.

Every morning I get up at 7:00.   I brush my teeth, and I clean my room.   I don't eat breakfast, but I drink coffee.   At 8:00 I walk to the drug store and I buy a newspaper.   I wait at the bus stop in front of the drug store and take the bus to work.

Yesterday I __*got*__ __*up*__ at 7:00.   I _____ my teeth, and I

_____ my room.   I _____ _____ breakfast, but I _____ coffee.   At 8:00

I _____ to the drug store and I _____ a newspaper.   I _____

at the bus stop, and I _____ the bus to work.

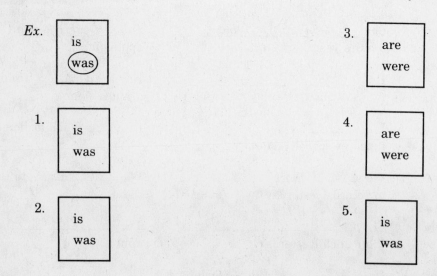

F. Listen to each sentence.   Put a circle around the word you hear.

Ex.
| is |
| (was) |

1.
| is |
| was |

2.
| is |
| was |

3.
| are |
| were |

4.
| are |
| were |

5.
| is |
| was |

136

TAPE SCRIPTS FOR LISTENING EXERCISES

Page 3   Exercise E

1. What's your phone number?
   My phone number is 231–4965.
2. What's your phone number?
   My phone number is 743–5296.
3. What's your phone number?
   My phone number is 492–7185.
4. What's your phone number?
   My phone number is 637–8976.

Page 3   Exercise F

1. 3
2. 8
3. 4
4. 7
5. 9
6. 6

Page 10   Exercise J

1. Where are they?   They're in the hospital.
2. Where are they?   They're in the supermarket.
3. Where's Mary?   She's in the bank.

Page 10   Exercise K

1. Where are you?
2. I'm in the car with Mrs. Jones.
3. Where's Mr. Jones?
4. He's in Mexico City.
5. Where are you?
6. I'm in the bathroom.
7. Where's the newspaper?
8. It's in the living room.

Page 16   Exercise D

1. The cat is in the garage.
2. What's she doing?
3. They're reading.
4. I'm playing the guitar.
5. He's listening.
6. You're in the cafeteria.
7. What are they doing?
8. He's in the classroom.

Page 19   Exercise D

1. 695–3352
2. 496–8577
3. 724–0681
4. 358–9677
5. 582–4196

Page 32   Exercise I

1. The movie theater is at 14 Main Street.
2. The cafeteria is at 19 Main Street.
3. The hospital is at 22 Main Street.
4. The library is at 27 Main Street.
5. The post office is at 28 Main Street.
6. The laundromat is at 31 Main Street.
7. The zoo is at 54 Central Street.
8. The supermarket is at 59 Central Street.
9. The restaurant is at 62 Central Street.
10. The bank is at 65 Central Street.
11. The night club is at 73 Central Street.

Page 33   Exercise K

1. In Moscow, it's 34°F/1°C.
2. In Cairo, it's 86°F/30°C.
3. In Caracas, it's 93°F/34°C.
4. In San Francisco, it's 72°F/22°C.
5. In Paris, it's 41°F/5°C.
6. In Athens, it's 68°F/20°C.
7. In Tokyo, it's 57°F/14°C.
8. In Rio de Janeiro, it's 98°F/37°C.

Page 42   Exercise C

1. There's a fire station between the hospital and the bank.
2. There's a police station next to the bank.
3. There's a gas station across from the fire station.
4. There's a train station around the corner from the gas station.
5. There's a school next to the gas station.
6. There's a drug store next to the school.
7. There's a church across from the drug store.
8. There's a cafeteria around the corner from the church.
9. There's a restaurant across from the cafeteria.
10. There's a movie theater across from the train station.
11. There's a clinic across from the bank.
12. There's a post office next to the clinic.
13. There's a supermarket around the corner from the drug store.
14. There's a library across from the supermarket.

Page 52   Exercise D

1. coats
2. cars
3. umbrella
4. exercise
5. dogs
6. shoe
7. dress
8. restaurants
9. necklaces
10. earrings
11. belt
12. watch
13. banks
14. houses
15. jackets
16. glove

Page 54   Exercise G

1. I'm washing these dresses.
2. She's reading these books.
3. I'm looking for this man.
4. He's cleaning this room.
5. He's fixing these refrigerators.

Page 54   Exercise H

1. This bicycle . . .
2. These exercises . . .
3. These apartments . . .
4. This car . . .
5. These women . . .
6. This necklace . . .
7. This house . . .
8. These shirts . . .

Page 60   Exercise F

1. These gloves . . .
2. This house . . .
3. This bicycle . . .
4. These stockings . . .

Page 66   Exercise G

Every day I sit in the park. I read the newspaper, I play cards, I eat my lunch, and I listen to the radio. I'm not a busy person.

My friend Harry lives around the corner from my house. Every day Harry cleans his apartment, he plays the piano, he reads books, he does exercises, and he cooks. My friend Harry is a very busy person.

Page 70   Exercise C

1. What kind of music does Mrs. Harris like?
2. Where do Gloria and Barbara study English?
3. Do Frank and Martha go to school?
4. Why do you go to Wilson's Department Store?
5. What does Mr. Larson do in the park?
6. Why do your aunt and uncle eat at Lee's Chinese Restaurant?
7. When does Mrs. Williams go to the bank?
8. What do the children do at the beach?
9. Does your sister do her homework?
10. When do you and your husband go to the supermarket?

Page 74   Exercise D

Ex. What kind of songs does Carmen Jones sing?
1. Do Bob and Judy go to school?
2. When does Mr. Johnson go to the park?
3. What do you do at school?
4. Where do John's cousins live?
5. Why do you go to Mario's Italian Restaurant?

Page 78   Exercise F

1. I usually listen to her.
2. I never read it.
3. I help him when I'm at school.
4. I always sit with them.
5. I play with him every day.
6. I don't like them.

Page 80   Exercise H

My grandmother has brown eyes and gray curly hair. She's short and heavy. She lives with us, and I'm very glad. Here's why I think she's wonderful.

When we go to parties, my grandmother always dances with me. When I talk to her, she always listens to me, and when my friends talk to her, she listens to them.

When I have difficult homework, my grandmother usually helps me. When I'm hungry, she always feeds me. When we eat together, she always talks to me, and when I'm upset, she always sits with me.

My grandmother is rarely upset. When our clothes are dirty, she washes them. When the sink is broken, she fixes it. When my little sisters are noisy, she plays with them.

My grandmother is really wonderful.

Page 88   Exercise G

JANE AND BETTY
1. Jane and Betty are looking for a restaurant. They're very hungry. They usually eat dinner at home, but their mother isn't cooking today.

JACK
2. Jack never does his homework. His teacher is always upset. Jack rarely helps his parents. He never washes the dishes, and he rarely washes the clothes. His parents are usually angry at him.

TOM
3. Tom is usually very happy. He loves his friends and his family, and he usually smiles at them. But today Tom isn't smiling. He's shouting at his little sister because she isn't studying.

VACATION
4. When my family and I are on vacation, I always have a wonderful time. I usually go to the beach, but when it's cold, I read books and listen to music. Today is a beautiful vacation day, and I'm playing tennis with my sister in the park.

Page 90   Exercise E

Ex. What are Fred and Jane doing today?
1. What do you usually do when you go to parties?
2. Where are you going today?
3. What does Robert usually do when he's nervous?
4. What kind of food does Mrs. Jones usually cook?
5. Is Henry fixing the car?

Page 92   Exercise D

1. My grandmother can speak Russian.
2. My sister can't sing.
3. My sister can't bake.
4. John and his brother can play checkers.
5. I can't drive a car.
6. My father can't play football.
7. Tommy can play the violin.
8. I can't drive a bus.
9. Can you cook Mexican food?
10. Mr. and Mrs. Johnson can ski.
11. They can't read Greek newspapers.
12. They can play soccer.

Page 102   Exercise F

TODAY'S WEATHER FORECAST
This is Tom Jones with today's weather forecast. This afternoon it's going to be warm and sunny with temperatures from 70° to 75°. This evening it's going to be cool and very cloudy, but it isn't going to rain.

THIS WEEKEND'S FORECAST
This is Nancy Peters with your weekend weather forecast. Tonight it's going to be foggy and cool with 50° temperatures, but on Saturday it's going to be clear and sunny. On Sunday wear your heavy clothes. It's going to be very cold.

MONDAY'S WEATHER FORECAST
This is Dan Richards with Monday's weather forecast. Monday morning it's going to be cool and cloudy, but wear your snow boots when you go to work because in the afternoon and evening it's going to snow. Tuesday's skiing is going to be wonderful. It's going to be sunny and cold.

Page 107   Exercise N

1. nine thirty
2. five o'clock
3. six fifteen
4. three forty-five
5. eight fifteen
6. half past two
7. seven fifteen
8. eleven forty-five
9. twelve o'clock
10. half past one
11. a quarter after three
12. four forty-five

Page 111   Exercise G

Every day at school I study English, mathematics, French, science, and music.   English class begins at 8:15.   I go to mathematics at 10:30.   I'm always happy at 11:45 because we have lunch.   We go to French class at 12:15.   We have science at 1:30 and we go to music at 2:45.

Page 112   Exercise B

Helen is home today with her family because her sisters and brothers are all sick. What's the matter with them?

1. Her brother David has a very bad headache.
   He feels terrible.
2. Her sister Patty isn't at school because she has a toothache.
3. Edward has a sore throat.
4. Alice is very upset because she has a backache.
5. What's the matter with Jack? He doesn't know, but he feels terrible.

Helen's family is sick today, but not Helen.

6. Helen feels fine.

Page 115   Exercise E

1. I study.
2. I studied.
3. I worked.
4. I work.
5. I wait for the train.
6. I waited for the bus.
7. I bake.
8. I cooked breakfast.
9. I played cards.
10. I play the piano.
11. I fixed the car.
12. I visited my friends.
13. I skate.
14. I rest.
15. I rested.

Page 121   Exercise B

   Sally is very tired today.   She worked all day yesterday, and her family didn't help her.   Yesterday morning she fixed the car.   Yesterday afternoon she painted the bathroom.   Yesterday evening she cleaned the basement.   She didn't rest all day.
   Sally's brother isn't very tired today.   Yesterday he didn't work.   He didn't fix the car.   He didn't paint the bathroom, and he didn't clean the basement.   What did he do?   He talked on the telephone all morning.   He listened to music all afternoon, and he rested in front of the TV all evening.

Page 124   Exercise G

1. When did Betty go to the bank?
2. What does Fred study at school?
3. When did Peter do his homework?
4. What did you buy at the store?
5. What kind of music do you listen to?

6. Who did he visit in Paris?
7. When does Nancy write to her grandmother?
8. Where did Alice and Jane play basketball?
9. When do Mr. and Mrs. Johnson go dancing?
10. When did Billy clean his room?

Page 127   Exercise C

1. Mary is happy today.
2. Mrs. Wilson was very busy today.
3. The children were very noisy this morning.
4. The weather was beautiful today.
5. John is very hungry this morning.
6. We were very tired this evening.
7. Sally's clothes are always dirty.
8. Anita and Carmen are very sick today.
9. My grandmother was never angry.
10. Our homework is very easy today.
11. My sister and I are very upset.
12. Nancy and Rita were at school today.

Page 132   Exercise H

A. How old were you when you met Grandmother?
B. I was twelve years old, and she was eleven.
A. Where did you meet?
B. We went to school together, and I sat next to your grandmother in science class.
A. Did you help her with her science homework?
B. No, I didn't.   She helped me.   She was a very good student, but I wasn't.

Page 132   Exercise I

A. Miss Gaylord.   What did you look like when you were a child?   Were you very beautiful?   Did you have many boyfriends?
B. My sisters were pretty, but I was short and heavy.   I had straight brown hair and freckles.   I didn't like boys, and they didn't like me.   When I went to parties, I was always embarrassed.

Page 133   Exercise J

A. How old was Tommy when he began to walk?
B. He was ten months old, and I bought him his first pair of shoes.   When he began to talk, his first words were "shoes" and "thank you."
A. Really?   Did I tell you about my grandson Jimmy?   He was eight months old when he began to walk.
B. Yes, you did, but that's okay.   I love to hear about Jimmy.   How old is he now?
A. He's twenty years old.

Page 136   Exercise F

Ex. Sally was very sad this morning.
1. My mother is very tired today.
2. Was Helen busy this morning?
3. John and Judy are very hungry this afternoon.
4. My aunt and uncle were at a concert.
5. Mr. Jones was late.

CORRELATION KEY

Note: A Correlation Key for this workbook may also be found in the Appendix of the *Side by Side* Core Conversation Course—Beginning Level.